Now I Know
Why Tigers
Eat Their Young

How to Order:

Single copies may be ordered from Prima Publishing, P.O. Box 1260BK, Rocklin, CA 95677; telephone (916) 786-0426. Quantity discounts are also available. On your letterhead, include information concerning the intended use of the books and the number of books you wish to purchase.

Now I Know Why Tigers Eat Their Young

Dr. Peter Marshall

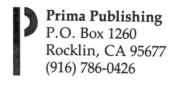
Prima Publishing
P.O. Box 1260
Rocklin, CA 95677
(916) 786-0426

Cover design by The Dunlavey Studio, Sacramento
Cover and interior illustration by Warren Clark

Library of Congress Cataloging-in-Publication Data
Marshall, Peter, 1947-
    Now I know why tigers eat their young: how to survive your teenagers — with wisdom and a little humor/Peter Marshall.
        p.   cm.
    Originally published: Whitecap Books, 1992.
    Includes bibliographical references and index.
    ISBN 1-55958-499-8 (pbk.)
    1. Parent and teenager—United States.   2. Parenting—United States.   I. Title.
HQ799.15.M37   1994
649'.125—dc20   93-48110
                                                                  CIP

94 95 96 97 RRD 10 9 8 7 6 5 4 3 2 1

Printed in the United States of America

*To Joanne and Tim, who survived their
teenage years without being eaten; Aaron, Kiera,
and Alexandra—may you enjoy the same fate;
and Kathy—may we grow old together
and not show it.*

Acknowledgments

I have learned that it is no easy matter to take an idea and transform it into a manuscript that a publisher might want to consider. Lorraine Greey provided the encouragement and advice I needed in my efforts to become an author. Her confidence in the project helped me to keep mine. She found a home for the book and asked for no more than a copy in return. There are some people it is hard to thank enough.

Sandi Porter took the time to review portions of the manuscript. It is always helpful to have the comments of the people whose opinions you can trust.

Nancy Knowles kept the practice going while I struggled to be both a psychologist and an author, and Judy Iocco and Veronica Willoughby saw me through the many revisions of the manuscript. Thank you.

I sometimes wonder why my wife puts up with me. She became virtually a single parent at home caring for the children while I was at the office writing about them. Although I was never tempted to change places, I owe a great deal to her. She was also my chief critic and reviewer throughout the preparation of the first draft. In a moment of weakness I promised to hand over the royalties; in truth, she has more than earned them.

Contents

Preface

IT HURT ME SOMEWHAT THAT EVEN AFTER EIGHTEEN years of practice in child psychology no one had asked me to write a book. I had lived with the secret hope that some day I would be begged to put pen to paper. Then I realized that to cling to the fantasy would only condemn me to disappointment. I stopped sulking and, without invitation, wrote this book secure in the knowledge that at least my mother would read it.

Raising teenagers is a serious business in many respects, but there is plenty of room for taking a light-hearted approach. Dealing with adolescents as they approach adulthood and strive for greater independence and control of their lives often leads to periods of tension and conflict in the home. While I have endeavored to treat the subject matter with the respect it deserves, I advocate humor as an essential defense mechanism and coping strategy for parents during this stage of their children's development.

When it comes to raising their teenagers, parents should see themselves as the real experts. The past two decades have seen a rapid increase in the number of publications about child-rearing, and I am adding one to the list. There is a risk, however, that parents will underestimate their own knowledge and skills; they can begin to believe that they have to study the collected works of psychologists and childcare specialists in order to learn the recipe for raising a successful, well-adjusted teenager. This recipe does not exist and is probably unattainable. By virtue of the professions we have chosen, however, we can offer to act as consultants. In this role, I present ideas and information on topics such as parenting styles, sex education, and self-esteem. My aim is to provide information and perspectives that parents will find useful in developing the expertise they already possess.

I have taken care to maintain an optimistic and positive tone. Notions such as the generation gap and adolescent rebellion can be exaggerated, and I address a number of the myths and misconceptions that can lead parents to dread the teenage years. This stage in family life can undoubtedly be stressful, but it is typically one that brings about many healthy and necessary changes in adolescents. The results from several studies support the conclusion that parents can take pride in the job they are doing of raising the next generation of young adults.

Research is often not discussed in books about teenagers. I have chosen to incorporate some of the work of social scientists and have tried to do so in a way that avoids the dryness of many academic articles and textbooks. The results of their studies can be useful, as they provide information that parents may want to consider when making decisions. Issues such as whether or not high-school students should have a part-time job or be exposed to sex education have been hotly debated. There are now sufficient data from research to help parents take a position on these and other matters.

My practice often finds me in the company of young people and their parents. I have the opportunity to hear about their struggles and complaints, as well as their successes and the steps they are taking to find solutions to the problems that brought them to my office. I have discussed some of their experiences, only changing sufficient details to ensure full confidentiality.

One reason for choosing to write about teenagers is more personal. I have helped to raise two of them, so I needed the therapeutic release. We have three more children and perhaps the book is also motivated by the need to prepare myself for the fact that their adolescence will be adding excitement to our middle age. I have made several references to our family and admit to thoroughly enjoying the opportunity to give a one-sided account of our home life. Let me introduce those members of the family who will either exact retribution or forgive me. They are my wife, Kathy, and our five children, Joanne and Tim (now adults), and Aaron, Kiera, and Alexandra.

ONE

Looking Back: Our Selective Memories

It's Time for an Autobiography

MANY PARENTS SEEM TO SUFFER FROM RETROGRADE AMnesia. This is a fancy term for loss of memory. It is often used to describe what can happen to a person's memory after an accident or trauma. Having a child can, of course, be either or both. Retrograde simply means "before," and amnesia—I forget what this means. Parents of teenagers are particularly prone to this disorder. In extreme cases they actually come to believe that they were born pillars of middle-class society and that the worst crimes they committed in their youth were pilfering cookies, after which they were so guilt-ridden that they confessed and insisted on being grounded for months.

I have not been blessed with retrograde amnesia. I remember all too well my childhood and the systematic onslaught this represented on my parents' sanity. "Me and the boys" found ways of entertaining ourselves that stretched the tolerance of the criminal code. (I would like to think that "me and the girls" carried on in much the same way, but I was singularly unsuccessful in this regard.) I would much prefer not to remember this period, but my mother refuses to let me forget. After all, it was she who said, "Peter, there are many paths to hell, but why did you have to choose all of them?" While I may have disagreed with her about many things, she was always a good judge of character.

Now, those of you who led blameless childhoods and never caused your parents one sleepless night should stop reading immediately. To the rest of you who have not completely repressed your growing-up years, I invite you to complete the following exercise. It has two parts. The first can be completed on your own. The second is shared with someone else. If you have a spouse, she or he could participate. If not, find someone of similar age who does not have a history of blackmail or extortion.

Part 1 is designed to stimulate your memory. Take pencil and paper and tackle the following questions.

(1) Name two things you and your parents argued about regularly.
(2) Did you ever get lectured by your parents because of your performance at school—or lack of it?
(3) What were five obscene words you knew and had used by the age of fifteen?
(4) Did you ever go to, or hold, a party without your parents' permission?
(5) At what age did you first try alcohol?
(6) What music did you listen to and what did your parents think of it?
(7) Did you ever hang around with friends that your parents disapproved of?
(8) What best described your room as a teenager:

(a) Suitable for a full-page spread in *Better Homes and Gardens*
(b) Borderline presentable
(c) Eligible to be declared a conservation area because of the rare forms of life flourishing in its corners

(9) Did you ever steal in the community or from your parents? (Yes, "borrowing" from the change on the dresser counts unless you have paid the money back with interest.)

(10) Name one job you were given by your parents that you knew was reasonable but that you complained about regularly.

(11) Did you ever argue about use of the family car? Did you do anything to (or in) the car that upset your parents, or would have upset them if they had known about it?

(12) Think of a time you lied or otherwise deceived your parents that they still don't know about (I dare you to tell them now).

(13) Did you ever experiment with street drugs, such as marijuana?

(14) Did you ever look at pornographic magazines?

(15) What is THE WORST THING you ever did as a teenager?

Part 2 is an exercise that is a great ice-breaker at workshops. It is based on observing my wife when she is with her siblings and old high-school friends. Kathy has two brothers and two sisters. Their father never read Benjamin Spock and his definition of permissiveness was giving them the choice between bowing and saluting when he came home. They also went to a Catholic school and in those days the nuns did not fool around when it came to instilling knowledge and correct behavior in their charges. Talking en route to your next class was a venial sin and any boy caught with his hands in his pockets was sent to the Grand Inquisitor. As a result, the children devoted much of their time and energy to finding ways to beat the system at home and school. Listening to them talk about what they got up to with one another or with their friends is quite an education. The best part of their reminiscing is observing my in-laws' reactions when they are treated to these trips down memory lane. As yet they have only been permitted to hear segments of the collective memoirs; you have to take such things very gently. At times they seem amused. On other occasions, however, they are clearly shocked. You can see signs of welling disapproval and you know that, if there were a way to ground a middle-aged son or daughter, they would find it.

So sit down together with your lists and take turns talking about what you were like as teenagers. Try to outdo one another. You will probably find that, once your partner has disclosed a few of his or her misdemeanors, it will feel safer to talk about your past with abandon. In no time at all it will be like you are being interviewed for a lead article in *True Confessions*.

Learning from Experience

SOMETIMES IT SEEMS AS IF TEENAGERS WASTE A LOT OF time discovering what we have known and have been trying to teach them for years. I have met parents who are open in discussing the problems they had themselves during their adolescence. Remembering their negative experiences makes them determined that their son or daughter will not make the same mistakes. I have no difficulty empathizing with them. The drive to protect our children and our wish that they not be hurt in any way are very strong. But I have come to appreciate that children cannot always learn through hearing about other people's experiences. It simply doesn't work. This seems to be true at all stages of development. One example with young children is the "lesson" of the importance of sharing. Not that long ago my youngest child, Alexandra, was playing with a friend's daughter. Both are toddlers. Inevitably tears and raw violence erupted over possession of the favorite toy of the moment. Feeling the pressure to demonstrate my child-rearing skills, I offered suggestions about taking turns that were met with looks that, roughly translated, said, "Tell someone who cares." Fortunately Alexandra eventually yawned, or at least opened her mouth wide enough that I could pretend she had. This permitted the lame, but often-used justification for antisocial behavior—"She's a bit cranky, you know, she needs a nap."

Alexandra and Jennifer may well become good friends. As they grow older they will discover that sharing can help them have a lot of fun. They may want to play school and will learn that, while they can do this on their own, cooperation allows them to have a teacher and a student who can act out imagined scenes. All this learning will probably take place with very little teaching from their parents. Discussing abstract ideas such as sharing is unlikely to have much impact—children need to experience the negative consequences of not sharing and the positive consequences of working more cooperatively.

The importance of learning through experience continues during middle childhood and adolescence, and I encourage parents to use their autobiographies as a means of recognizing how much they also learned through trial-and-error. I like to join in such discussions. We often agree that we came to appreciate the need to be careful when forming friendships through having made some bad choices. Some of our assertiveness may only have developed after having experienced how unpleasant it feels to allow yourself to be dominated or manipulated by others. Like a number of teenagers I have seen, I needed to discover for myself that not having a high-school diploma closed too many doors before I appreciated the value of education.

It would be so much easier if they would simply listen and learn. If you are very lucky, your daughter or son may be a highly reflective and open person who will consider, analyze, and then accept much of your advice. I have tried to get such a teenager, but I am told they have been back-ordered for years. For most of us, learning through experience is necessary; it is also a powerful way of acquiring ideas and values, as it is based on real, rather than imagined, consequences.

Remembering Your Past
as an Alternative to Tranquilizers

ONE ASPECT OF WRITING ONE'S AUTOBIOGRAPHY THAT I find interesting is the comparison between myself as a teenager and how I am as a man in my forties. Certainly there are some similarities, but the differences are more compelling. If I had presented a panel of experts with a profile of myself at sixteen and asked for an objective opinion regarding my chances of becoming a reasonably stable and productive member of society, I am doubtful I would have been rated an odds-on favorite. In a similar vein, it is not uncommon for parents to tell me, "I know he'll turn out all right," but to say it in such a way that you know they are having a very hard time believing it.

This is where retrograde amnesia exerts such a strong influence. I can remember the outrage and fear that were elicited from many parents in the early sixties at the sight of the beatniks and hippies. While I and many of my generation grew our hair below our ears, listened to the Beatles and Rolling Stones, and wrote poetry with no punctuation, our parents watched with horror, lamented our impending doom, and thought, "There goes the human race." Somehow I believe we survived reasonably well and have not turned out too badly.

"But," I have heard, "the music is different now." Maybe, but I am not so sure it really is. I know, for example, that there is a heavy metal song entitled "Anal Vapors." It is not the sort of song I would want to include in a sing-along and it wouldn't be my choice for dinner music. But wasn't it the Beatles who asked the question, "Why don't we do it in the road?" They never told us what "it" was, but I doubt they were referring to soccer. And the Fab Four tell us on the Sergeant Pepper's album about someone who went into a dream, having gone upstairs to "have a smoke." I will never be convinced that was a reference to Players Light.

The nonconformists of the present generation may shave their heads; those of our generation did not shave at all. They may now dress in black; in the fifties and sixties tight pants, miniskirts, and pointed shoes all served to liven up the relationships between teenagers and parents. Future generations will no doubt find new and exciting ways to be different and shocking. This is a necessary separation device, and there is some solace in knowing that it almost guarantees that your grandchildren will repay your son or daughter in full for all the aggravation you endured.

I am not attempting to dismiss parental concerns regarding their adolescents as a sign of either neurosis or hypocrisy. Teenagers do need to have parents who are watching out for them and who will try to steer them away from situations that are likely to be damaging. Taking the time to recall our own experiences as teenagers, however, can be an enjoyable process that makes it easier to maintain a realistic and less worrying perspective on our adolescents' behavior.

TWO
Growth and Development

So Who Invented Teenagers Anyway?

IT CAME AS A SURPRISE TO ME TO LEARN THAT TEENAG-ers as we know and love them today did not always exist. I have wondered if this is what my grandmother meant when she reminded us that things were better in the "good old days." Like most of us, I have always seen teenagers as being in a separate stage of development—truly in a class all of their own. Prior to the mid-eighteenth century, however, a very different view prevailed. Children, let alone teenagers, were not seen as a distinct group. They were viewed as mini-adults who were expected to behave as such as soon as possible. For example, crawling was not seen as the milestone it is today. Rather, the sight of one's offspring crawling on the floor was more likely to be viewed as animal-like behavior that should be promptly corrected. Special clothes were even designed that kept children in a rigid, adult-like posture as soon as they were able to stand.

Very young children did, in fact, function as mini-adults. Until the advent of child labor laws, which mostly came into effect in the latter part of the nineteenth century, children who in our day and age would be attending kindergarten could be employed full-time. In the London of Dickens's time they might be washing bottles or sweeping chimneys. They might also be working the land or employed as domestic servants.

It must have seemed quite a formidable task to take a newborn child and have him or her ready for the working world in as few as five or six years. Given the short period of time allotted to create a fully functional mini-adult, it would have been hard not to have a generally intolerant attitude towards the inevitable childish behaviors of one's offspring. Because they were seen as deviating so much from the model of adulthood, young children were often viewed very negatively. A common belief was that they were basically bad and in need of very strict discipline in order to bring them into line quickly.

I love reading authors who wrote about children during the past few centuries. One writer, Samuel Springer, stated with conviction that "all children have wicked hearts when they are born. Even little infants that appear so innocent and pretty are God's little enemies." This quote came to mind when I was looking through the glass screen at the nursery on the maternity ward where my last child was born. Viewing times usually bring a steady stream of onlookers and admirers who comment with pleasure and affection about the little bundles. I began wondering, however, about how Sam would have reacted if he had been there. I had a picture of him breaking into a cold sweat at the sight of the Satanic hoard and urging us to see beyond their sweet expressions and into the evil of their hearts.

Mr. Springer was not alone in his views. A clergyman is reputed to have pronounced that "as innocent as children seem to be, they are young vipers. They are infinitely more hateful than vipers and are in a most miserable condition. They are naturally very senseless and stupid and need much to awaken them." Parents were encouraged to share this opinion with their children. "Why should we conceal the truth from them?" he asked. Honest feedback from parents in those days wouldn't have done wonders for a child's self-esteem.

One short description of children from that era is a particular favorite of mine. The person who referred to children as "curly, dimpled lunatics" may have been overstating his case, but I suspect he was a parent who was just having a particularly bad day and was viewing a childless marriage as a golden but missed opportunity.

The notion that children should be seen as qualitatively different from adults began to gain ground in the nineteenth century. Writers started talking about childhood as a distinct stage of development. This was an important shift; once you start recognizing that children have different capabilities and needs, you become less inclined to refer to them as vipers or lunatics when they do not behave like adults. Furthermore, by the turn of the century childhood was being divided into separate stages and the concept of adolescence was born.

The shifts in thinking that occurred in society were not just the result of idle speculation or armchair theorizing. Probably a major reason for separating adolescence from childhood and adulthood was the industrial revolution. One spin-off had been a rapid decrease in the need for child labor and, before too long, more and more young people were staying in school rather than joining the work force. As a result, people began to see the teenage years as a phase during which the adolescent was being gradually prepared to meet the demands of the adult world.

I will give you the name of the person responsible for "inventing" adolescence, but just in case you are thinking of banding together and initiating a class action suit, he is no longer around to face the consequences of his actions. Dr. Stanley Hall died almost seventy years ago. A prominent psychologist, he devoted two volumes to the stage of adolescence, which he saw as beginning at roughly the age of twelve and continuing into the early twenties. He wrote about many aspects of development in this stage, covering topics such as physical changes, adolescent love, and intellectual development. In case you are wondering why he needed two volumes to discuss adolescence, he decided to include a section on "juvenile faults." I'm sure you can appreciate that it would have been hard to stop writing once he got going on this one.

Adolescence as a stage has remained part of society's thinking throughout this century. Our expectations regarding adolescents, however, have changed dramatically. The early view was primarily that they were to be molded; like sponges, they should soak up the truth and wisdom imparted by adults. However appealing this philosophy might be, it didn't seem to catch on with teenagers; they have insisted on having their own culture and identity. In recent years, for example, teenagers have become one of the most important consumer groups. Their tastes, interests, and preferences are studied carefully by market researchers. They have their own fashions, music, and literature. They also have a political identity and there have been eras such as the Vietnam war when they have become loud and powerful voices for change.

It made good sense to extend the period allowed for young people to develop. In our highly literate, industrial, and technological world it takes much longer to become educated. An obvious consequence is that the period of dependency on parents has increased. So have the demands on parents to take responsibility for assisting their children through this lengthy transitional phase during which so many important changes occur.

Physical Growth

THE PITUITARY GLAND HAS A LOT TO ANSWER FOR. IT IS no bigger than a pea, but it packs a punch to be reckoned with. Known as a "master gland," it gets the other glands going, secreting the hormones that are either directly or indirectly responsible for many of the changes that occur in adolescence. And unfortunately you can't check your kids in to have it taken out, like you can tonsils when they become troublesome. It is tucked away at the base of the brain, well-hidden and protected.

There are many changes that will occur in the body during adolescence. One of the most obvious is the rapid increase in height, referred to as the growth spurt. Weight also increases, as does the amount of both fatty and muscle tissue. You now find yourself looking at a son or daughter who has lost that childlike appearance and has very quickly acquired an unmistakably adult build.

Major changes take place in the brain. One statistic I love is that adolescent brains use only half the energy of those belonging to younger children. I used this fact to convince my teenagers that they were dealing with only half a deck. (I confess I never gave them the full story. The drop in energy consumption continues throughout adulthood, but I saw no reason to overwhelm them with information.)

The sex glands and reproductive organs are another target for growth and development. These aspects of maturation form the period we know as puberty, which is discussed in the chapter on sexuality.

There are a number of aspects of physical development that have particular relevance for adolescents psychologically. While the glands and hormones responsible for the changes seem to get the job done eventually, they do not coordinate their efforts very well. The term "asynchrony" is often used here. It refers to the fact that growth in different parts of the body does not proceed at a consistent, uniform pace. One illustration is the very rapid increase in the size of the hands and feet. For a number of teenagers it is almost as if they have woken up one morning to find that their limbs have become longer. During the period that the brain and the rest of the body are learning how to adjust to having longer limbs, the teenager will seem to be clumsy and gangly and will go through a period in which he is well-advised to stay away from china stores and take a temporary break from tap-dancing classes. Not surprisingly, the fact that growth is rapid and uneven makes many adolescents feel awkward and self-conscious.

It is also established that the process of physical maturation begins at an earlier age than was the case in previous centuries. Although the reason for this is not known for sure, improvement in nutrition and health care may well be a major factor. This leaves us with two trends that are in exactly opposite directions. At the same time that society is prolonging adolescence, nature is speeding up the process of becoming physically mature. As a result we have young people whom we view very much as children who often see themselves as far more grown up and mature than we do.

There has been interest in studying the impact of the age of onset of physical maturation. While it is typically earlier than in previous generations, it varies a great deal from child to child. For boys, early onset of physical maturation is a plus. Being successful athletically still offers greater status for boys than girls, and having their bodies mature will often give them an advantage in competitive sport. In comparison to late developers, the early bloomers are also more likely to be seen as attractive to girls and are in a better position to be selected for leadership roles. For their peers whose hormones are not so quick off the mark, life can be more frustrating. They are often seen as generally less mature and less able to take on adultlike responsibilities. They are also more likely to see themselves negatively and, perhaps as a means of compensating for these feelings of inadequacy, can become rebellious and noncompliant. (A word of caution: if you have a twelve-year-old son, do not start slipping growth hormones into his orange juice just because he hasn't started shaving. While it is true that late developers tend to find adolescence more frustrating, they typically survive just fine. Many other factors are relevant here. A late bloomer who has a supportive family and has established a circle of close friends will not suffer that much, even if he has to endure periods of ribbing in the changing room.)

For girls, the situation is more complicated. Early maturation is generally a disadvantage in the younger age group. Girls who are well into puberty in grade six or sooner often feel very self-conscious and are embarrassed by their precocious development. By grade seven or eight, however, being physically mature offers definite prestige and it is the late developer who is more dissatisfied with her body and is likely to be experiencing anxiety and self-doubt relating to lack of development.

The bodily changes have a substantial impact on the adolescent's self-concept. Girls worry about the shape and size of their breasts and become particularly concerned about their facial characteristics, skin, and hair. Boys tend to be preoccupied with the size and strength of their bodies. The increase in the size of the penis is also a very important matter for them.

Once again, sex differences emerge. Overall, adolescent girls experience greater dissatisfaction regarding their bodies; this, we assume, is a product of the stereotyping that has conditioned girls to place excessive value on their physical appearance. In one study, students were asked to rate both the attractiveness and effectiveness of their bodies. The girls who rated their bodies as being more attractive to others were found to have more positive self-concepts. Boys were different. It was the perceived effectiveness of their bodies more than physical attractiveness that was associated with greater self-esteem.

I am reminded that, even though my adolescence was far from being the most content and settled period of my life, I was lucky in many respects. I think my hormones were a bit on the heavy side. I quickly developed hairy legs, but never needed the fingers of both hands to count the hairs on my chest. As it happened, this was not a problem. I was in the school pipe band and every Friday I wore my kilt, my legs proudly displaying the proof of my emerging manhood. Still, I can remember how often we seemed to discuss and worry about the relative status of our physical development. We wanted our voices to break, boasted about an increase in shoe size, and scoured our faces for any sign of growth that would justify the purchase of a razor.

Wonderful though it might be, I would like to see some design changes in the human body. If I had been consulted I would have recommended a far more gradual period of change. I would also have insisted on not having the broad range of differences between children in the onset and pace of adolescence. After all, in many areas we routinely group children quite rigidly on the basis of chronological age. The school system is one obvious example. My wife teaches grade seven and knows only too well the problems associated with having a group that, while consisting of young people of similar age, contains some who physically resemble young children and others who are capable of having children of their own. The speed and variability of physical growth and development may not present major difficulties for all adolescents, but for some they can create a period of insecurity and self-doubt.

The Age of Reason?

THIS IS THE RISKY PART OF THE CHAPTER, WHEN ANY credibility I may have gained could be totally lost and you will be convinced that psychologists should stick to running rats through mazes. One of the most important and dramatic changes that takes place in adolescents is that they become capable of sophisticated and rational thinking. While I am the first to acknowledge that, at times, it may seem that teenagers have left, rather than entered, an age of reason, I assure you this is not the case. I would also like to try to convince you that much of the insecurity and conflict that can be experienced by teenagers is, in fact, the result of their ability to think in different and more complex ways.

Take moral development, for example. Very young children have a notion of good or bad that is determined largely by external rewards and punishments rather than any internal moral code. They are very quick to recognize how people react to their behavior and sensing disapproval can be sufficient punishment. At this stage, however, something is bad because it leads to a negative consequence, not because they feel it is basically wrong. As they get older, children internalize rules and standards—usually those of their parents and other important people in their lives. This acceptance is not, however, based on any thinking about underlying moral or ethical principles; the children simply adopt the prevailing party-line.

As they develop the capacity to think in more complex terms, children begin to focus on the principles and ideas underlying a particular rule. For example, they may have been taught that it is wrong to hit other people. They will automatically apply this principle and see behavior such as bullying in the schoolyard as bad. As adolescents, they may examine the more abstract idea that it is morally wrong to use physical force to solve problems. This can make life more complicated. If the reason bullying is unacceptable is that force is being used to dominate other children, why is it all right for societies to have armed military and police forces? Debating this, and other issues, can lead teenagers to doubt, question, and challenge many of the ideas and beliefs they have held.

The same capacity for complex reasoning will influence the development of other areas of life. One psychologist, Joseph Adelson, devised an interesting approach to studying political thinking. He asked subjects in his studies to imagine that a group of one thousand people bought an island. The task was then to describe how this new society should be organized. He found that, unlike younger children, adolescents demonstrated understanding of broad concepts, such as justice and equality, which they applied when creating their island society.

The role of adolescents as a political force in our society has been touched on briefly earlier in this chapter. This was clearly evident in the sixties when the peace movement gained momentum in many parts of the world. While the current generation may not have such a high profile politically, I would not underestimate its power and influence. Teenagers' interest in the environment provides an illustration. Every so often we hear reports of high-school groups pressuring the catering companies to eliminate unnecessary packaging and disposable cutlery and provide recycling bins. Discussions regarding plastic knives and forks and pop cans may be less newsworthy than debates on the arms race, but like many others, I have come to believe that young people's developing concerns regarding how individuals and societies treat the environment will prove to be of immense value in ensuring our future welfare.

Religious values are also likely to be influenced by the changes in thinking capacity. Once again, the process is often one of questioning—of not automatically assuming that a viewpoint is correct simply because you have been brought up with it. The adolescent can become acutely aware of how many people subscribe to quite different religious beliefs and can find it an interesting intellectual endeavor to compare philosophies.

A whole chapter has been devoted to self-esteem, as it seems to be such a critical aspect of adolescent development. Just as teenagers can engage in more sophisticated thinking about the outside world, so their thinking about themselves can show greater range and depth. They start considering what it would be like to have different personalities. For example, a teenager may wonder whether or not she should be more assertive. She is able to imagine a variety of situations involving herself and others and weigh the pros and cons of being more assertive. If she decides the outcome would be favorable, she may change her personality in this way.

The process of deciding the kind of person one wants to be leads to the development of the ideal self. Creating this ideal version is important as it provides a goal to strive for. It can also be frustrating. It is like trying to keep to New Year's resolutions. Most of us have to renew these annually: our attempts at self-improvement rarely last beyond mid-February. Inevitably, therefore, there will be a discrepancy between the ideal self and the real self.

After forty years of living with them, I have become accustomed to my imperfections. I have also had the benefit of loved ones who, while not shy about reminding me of my shortcomings, display remarkable tolerance for them. As a result, my ideal and real selves seem to get along quite well, in spite of their differences. In early adolescence, however, the task of living with different versions of the self can become a major struggle. For example, our teenager with the goal of being more assertive may become very frustrated when she finds out how hard it can be to stand up for what she thinks and wants. For many young adolescents, this conflict between who they are and who they want to be is probably one of the reasons why their self-esteem is relatively low.

I expect that most psychologists would agree that the changes that take place in the adolescent's ability to think and reason are one of the most important stages of maturation. At the same time, this stage is often one of the least evident. After all, outgrowing your clothes in a matter of months, having your voice break, or developing breasts are changes that are obviously noticeable and will inevitably elicit the "my, how fast you are growing up" comment from relatives. Intellectually, adolescents are also leaving childhood rapidly, although this departure takes place with little public awareness or fanfare.

The Storm and Stress Theory

"MOODY" AND "UNPREDICTABLE" ARE ADJECTIVES PARents often use when referring to their teenagers. They can be excited and happy one moment and in deep despair or just plain miserable the next. Stanley Hall coined the term "storm and stress" to describe these swings of emotion. His theory was that, because of all the changes taking place, adolescence was inevitably a period of much tension, conflict, and turbulence. Even though this notion became popular among psychologists, it has not been supported by the research. Contrary to Hall's prediction, it seems that only a minority of teenagers go through a lengthy period of instability.

Failure to find general support for the notion of "storm and stress" does not, however, mean that the adolescent years are supposed to be smooth or that you are alone if you have secretly sent off for brochures on boarding schools in the Arctic Circle. There is no doubt that most adolescents do experience a faster and more dramatic rate of change in their moods than adults. An interesting way of studying these mood fluctuations was developed by two social scientists, Mihaly Czikszentmihalyi and Reed Larson. They provided teenagers with pagers and proceeded to contact them at random to find out what they were doing and how they were feeling. (I wish I had thought of this first. I would have paged them at ten on a Friday night and seven on Sunday morning; the first time out of curiosity and the second for revenge.) It was found that some, but by no means all, of the teenagers experienced dramatic fluctuations in mood over relatively brief periods of time. An important finding was that these fluctuations did not seem to indicate psychological difficulties. The teenagers who had the greatest mood swings seemed to be as much in control of their lives and appeared equally as well-adjusted as their more even-tempered counterparts. Doubtlessly they were less fun to live with, but it seems it was their parents' sanity, rather than their own, that was being threatened.

You are also far from alone if you feel that arguing has become your teenager's favorite pastime. We actually have detailed statistics on this topic. On average, high-school students become involved in .35 arguments a day. The average length of the argument is eleven minutes. (I did not keep records, but I think my first two children—now grown up—overindulged themselves and used up their quotas by the age of fifteen.) The arguments are most frequently in the home and involve both siblings and parents. When they occur between teenagers and parents, the majority involve mothers and daughters.

The conflicts between parents and teenagers certainly add nothing to the quality of life. My brother and I spent most of our adolescent years making sure that any love between us was well and truly masked by running warfare. When we weren't arguing with each other, we were often disputing one of the house rules. How clearly I recall my mother looking at us and stating with conviction, "I should have had goldfish instead."

Just as mood fluctuations are not usually a sign of any serious psychological problem, conflict between parents and teenagers does not necessarily seem to be unhealthy. Some psychologists have even argued that, in moderation, conflict can be beneficial as a means of helping teenagers separate from their parents. This could, of course, be rampant rationalization, but I take some comfort in believing that all of the grief may have been worth it.

Rates of Change: Theirs and Ours

FOR THE ADOLESCENT, SO MUCH CHANGES WITHIN SUCH a brief period of time. In an effort to remain sensitive to how rapidly my teenagers were developing I used to compare their pace of life with my own. In one short year my son began driving and had his first girlfriend, job, and hangover. The highlights of my year were turning forty, winning a ham in a raffle, and becoming vice-president of the P.T.A. As far as I was concerned, I had a good year, but there was simply no contest when it came to deciding whose life was more exciting and memorable.

The different rates of change between parents and teenagers can make life stressful at times. After all, it's much easier to live with people when they are changing at a similar rate. When I think of my marriage, for example, I acknowledge that both Kathy and I are, in many ways, not the people we were when we embarked on life's journey together. My version is that she has become more mellow and reasonable, while I have come even closer to the pinnacle of perfection. Her version might be quite different, but this is my book. Although the changes have not occurred in the absence of conflict (believe me, they have not) we have had the time to gradually accommodate to one another. By comparison, the rate of change in my children during their adolescence was so much faster and seemed much harder to accept and accommodate.

Keeping pace with our teenagers' development is not easy. Theirs is a stage of dramatic physical and psychological change and, while childhood may have been extended by our society, the period from the onset of adolescence to adulthood only spans a few years. Because of our different rates of change, we may see them as inconsistent, impulsive, and unstable; in their eyes we may be staid, boring, and much too predictable.

THREE

Parenting Styles

What is a Parenting Style?

I DOUBT THAT MANY OF US THINK OF OURSELVES AS HAV-
ing adopted a particular style of parenting. We certainly have
values and attitudes that are important to us and we incorporate
these into our dealings with our children. We have opinions
regarding how much control they should be given and probably
have our own way of establishing rules and consequences. Some of
our rules come from books and some from remembering how we
were raised as children. We borrow ideas from parents we know
and we use our creativity to help us develop an approach to family
life that seems to fit for us. Given that few of us have a set recipe to

follow, or would be able to follow one if we did, each family can, in many respects, be seen as unique. By comparison, psychologists usually refer to only a small number of parenting styles. I have limited myself to four. This can seem somewhat at odds with the view that families are unique. Trying to pigeonhole every family into one of the categories or styles would, in fact, be an impossible task and probably not a sensible one to undertake in the first place. I cannot look at my own family, for example, and conclude we belong to any one category.

So why talk about parenting styles? It is a useful way of focusing on some of the more critical aspects of the approaches or philosophies we bring to family life. Like many parents, I believe, for example, that issues regarding who should be in control, the extent to which family rules are negotiated, and how communication is developed are very important and need to be addressed frequently throughout the course of children's development. Describing different styles provides a way of highlighting the various ways these issues can be addressed. Each style consists of a set of attitudes and values that will influence the way parents see both their own roles and responsibilities and those of their children. These attitudes and values will also have a direct influence on how we actually behave towards our children.

Authoritarian Style

THE AUTHORITARIAN STYLE OF PARENTING IS THE ONE usually held up as an example of what not to do. Authoritarian parents give orders and expect immediate obedience. They set very rigid rules and only they have the right to change them. Their children are supposed to passively follow directions and never question the parents' right to govern. Should the children dare to question their absolute authority, they are immediately assumed to be rebellious and disrespectful and in urgent need of punishment. Negotiation simply is not a term in the authoritarian parent's vocabulary.

I have met many employers who would readily match the above description, as would numerous politicians around the world. Actually, speaking as a parent, the authoritarian style has a certain appeal. It would definitely make life a lot easier. It is a statement of fact that, if everyone in my family would do exactly as I want them to do, things would run much more smoothly.

At this point I suppose I should be slamming the authoritarian style of parenting, listing all the problems it is supposed to cause. I will get to that later, but for now I want to dwell on the merits of being a benign dictator. I can certainly agree that dictators and teenagers rarely enjoy good relationships and that authoritarian approaches to child-rearing need to be modified greatly during the adolescent years. But this raises the question of why the authoritarian approach might have developed in the first place. I work on the assumption that most of us are semirational and that, unless proven otherwise, our behavior reflects at least a smattering of good sense.

If you look at the first few years of life, how much room is there for discussion and flexibility? I have never "negotiated" a diaper change, and seeing a toddler about to determine whether or not a spoon can be inserted into an electrical outlet has never prompted me to explore choices with them. Having young children in bed by a certain time is not, in my opinion, a flexible matter. Rather, it is one of the safeguards I take to preserve what is left of my sanity. If my child wants to tell me why she dislikes school, I will probably listen sympathetically. But if she tells me she wants to quit at the end of grade three and embark on a career washing bottles or sweeping chimneys, I will break the news to her that she was born a hundred and fifty years too late and ensure that she is on the school bus the next day.

We do not give young children many choices. In fact, infants get none. When children begin to use language, we may take the time to try to explain why we do what we do. But make no mistake, we are going to do it no matter what.

When I talk in this vein to parents, a number will insist that they often give their young children choices. I used to believe that I did. What convinced me of my error was taking the time to observe myself in action with my children and make a note of examples of my "negotiating."

When my son was four, one of his favorite forms of entertainment was to kick his baby sister under the table during meal times. I think this was Aaron's first major experience with the lawful nature of the universe. He learned quickly that even a gentle tap guaranteed a loud screech from Kiera. Of course, Aaron insisted he never kicked his sister. He tried to convince us that these incidents were accidents caused by the random motor activity in his legs. The observation that these "accidents" were always accompanied by a broad grin on his face left no doubt, however, as to the truth of the matter.

All of us value peace at the dinner table, so I decided to enter into negotiations with Aaron. "You have a choice. You can either stop kicking your sister or you can sit on the stairs. You will be sitting on the stairs until bath time and you won't get any dessert. What would you like to do?" Now I suppose that could be seen as a choice. After all, I did not tell him he had to stop kicking Kiera. But this reasoning is suspect. An example in the adult world would be an employer saying "Marshall, you have a choice. You can either undertake this assignment or you can empty your desk and collect your vacation pay on the way out."

Over the course of several weeks, the list of so-called choices grew longer. Aaron was told he could choose between not spraying his sister with the garden hose and sitting on the stairs, putting his toys away and sitting on the stairs, apologizing to his sister for calling her a "do-do head" and sitting on the stairs, and not using his sister as a toy submarine when they were together in the bath and sitting on the stairs. (You may have noticed certain patterns. First of all, Aaron certainly seemed to have opinions about his sister that we did not share. Also, we lacked imagination when it came to the second part of each choice. How people who live in bungalows or apartments cope with children is beyond my comprehension.)

Maybe we don't give children as many choices as we believe we do. And maybe we shouldn't. During adolescence there will also be situations in which choices are not given. Rules such as no drinking, having to comply with a curfew, and not swearing may not be negotiable. There may be some room for the teenager to have input into the nature of the rule, but the parents will insist that one is established. An important part of being a parent is having the confidence and assertiveness to provide clear expectations and standards for behavior and to insist that our children follow the rules. I see these features of the authoritarian style as assets. Of course, if a parent knows only how to be authoritarian and arbitrary, they can expect to have problems, particularly as their children enter adolescence. I will discuss the disadvantages of being overly authoritarian in a moment; for now I simply want to make the point that parents start the process of child-rearing by having extensive and arbitrary control over their offspring. Hopefully, we will exercise this power wisely, but I see no reason why it should ever be given up completely. As one of the modern leaders in family therapy, Salvador Minuchin, has stated, "The challenge of adolescence is to balance the right of the parents to feel they are in charge with the need of the adolescent to gain independence."

Now to the problems. If the authoritarian style is adhered to rigidly, it is very difficult for children to develop the skills and self-confidence needed to cope with the adult world. They do not learn to negotiate. Asserting their opinions in a reasonable way, while at the same time listening carefully to others' viewpoints, is not a process with which they are familiar. Rather, they are brought up believing that much of what goes on between people is a battle in which there will be a winner and a loser; someone has to prevail and dominate. Ideas are not debated and opinions are not sought from others. Children raised in this way are likely to see the world in black and white and this rigidity breeds intolerance. Compromise is not a word in their vocabulary.

We know from research that the children in authoritarian

families have little self-reliance. It is hardly surprising that they have difficulty thinking for themselves when they have learned from experience that their opinions do not count for much and have little, if any, influence on what happens. We also know that they are likely to be distrustful; they tend to view relationships as a struggle for power and control. They may be rebellious; on the other hand, they may be passive and submissive. Either way, they are more likely to be unhappy people who lack a view of themselves as competent and worthwhile.

Before panic sets in, you have not necessarily condemned your child to psychological purgatory if, in the last week, you have responded to her "Why should I?" with "Because I said so." What the research has told us, however, is that, if we do not encourage our children to voice their opinions and become part of the decision-making process in the family, they will suffer as a consequence. Sometimes parents hope that emphasizing obedience will encourage their children to be respectful. It might, but there is a real risk it will breed resentment and a lack of respect—both for themselves and others.

Management By Guilt

MANAGEMENT BY GUILT (MBG) IS A FORM OF PSYCHO-logical warfare. For the child it is like having to live with Dear Abby and Miss Manners at the same time. The hallmark of MBG is a facade of freedom. The children are conned into believing they can make up their own minds about all sorts of things. The parents will state their own preferences, but will not forbid their children to go against their wishes. Consequently, there is no obvious punishment imposed if the suggestions (not rules) are ignored.

But there's a catch. Going against the wishes of MBG parents carries a huge price. Children will be made aware (repeatedly) of how much damage they are doing to themselves and others. Good MBG parents are excellent nonverbal communicators. With no more than a brief glance and a faint sigh they can communicate how hurt and disappointed they are. They don't have to be asked what they think when they read a report card. The way they hand it back expresses all too well how they have worked so hard all these years just to make sure their children can have a good education and how they have let them down miserably by failing to become the star pupils of the school.

Seasoned MBG parents rarely, if ever, get angry at their offspring directly. If children do get a lecture, it is most likely to be an updated report on how the life span of loved ones is being shortened by their behavior. They are told, for example, that they are at liberty to go to the family reunion with safety pins through their cheeks, but warned that granddad's pacemaker may not withstand the strain.

Another hallmark of the MBG style is overgeneralization. The parents look at one particular event or behavior and automatically make sweeping generalizations. The punk hairdo serves as a worthy illustration. Now, I can appreciate why parents lack enthusiasm about being seen in public with a son or daughter who resembles a blend of a porcupine and a rainbow. The parents' concerns, however, go far beyond the lack of esthetic appeal of the hairstyle. Rather, they present it as irrefutable proof that their offspring has begun the slow slide into the abyss of sin and degradation. They are truly worried that all their attempts to instill moral values in their child have been fruitless and that they have, therefore, failed miserably. I do not doubt that their concern is genuine; they are caring people who are beginning to believe that their efforts to be good parents have come to nothing. But more often than not I look at the young person in question and get the impression of just a regular kid with a funny-looking head.

I do not want to imply that families come to see me because they are concerned only about hairstyles. Typically, there are several areas of conflict that are upsetting everybody. But what sometimes emerges is that these problems are not that severe or unusual. The tendency to overgeneralize, however, can transform a reason for concern into a cause for alarm and panic. Punk hairdos, listening to heavy-metal music, and multiple earrings become signs of being in league with Satanic forces. A single hickie is viewed much like a positive pregnancy test and a beer cap found in the waste basket justifies the diagnosis of alcoholism.

MBG parents also share some of the rigidity of the authoritarian style. But there is a difference. An authoritarian parent tends to say "This is the only way because I say so." The MBG parent's viewpoint is "This is the only way because this is what society expects." The goal is to ensure that the child conforms to the standards and expectations of others who are held in high esteem, such as neighbors, teachers, friends, or relatives. The child is taught to be very sensitive to their opinions: "What will so-and-so think if you do this?" is a question heard frequently in one form or another.

A feature of this style is "parenting by comparison." Other young people are presented as paragons of virtue and shining examples to follow. The skilled MBG parent has a readily available repertoire of "Why can't you be like......?" questions and an extensive list of names that can be inserted in the blank. These names are used carefully and selectively. When the issue is school work, the parents insert the names of students who have a permanent place on the honor roll. When discussing chores, they can cite examples of young people they know who willingly rise at six on weekends to vacuum the house, do the laundry, and mow the lawns. Somehow it is usually the case that those held up as models and standards are among the leading contenders for the "most disliked person" award; parents rarely compare their offspring to people they would see as "cool."

I hope no one working with families would ever maintain that parents should not set standards for their children. Problems tend to arise, however, when MBG is used frequently. As can happen in authoritarian families, the young person does not readily develop self-reliance. Excessive concern regarding other people's opinions can breed a self-consciousness and anxiety that inhibits psychological and social growth. Adolescents can spend too much time worrying about how they look to the rest of the world and become preoccupied with trying to secure approval from others. If they don't rebel they may become excellent conformers, but it is unlikely they will have a strong sense of their own identity or values.

I have found it very interesting and helpful to talk to adults who have been raised in MBG families. Twenty or thirty years can have passed, but they still have vivid memories of how they often felt they had failed to live up to the standards their parents set for them. What has made a particular impression on me is the extent to which they seem to be stuck in the past. It is as if they are still trying to prove something to their parents. Lodged firmly inside them is the belief that they are just not quite good enough; it is like a family version of original sin.

Several years ago I helped run a number of assertiveness training groups—the type of group where you learn how to return defective merchandise to department stores and stop people pushing in front of you in movie lineups without resorting to primitive forms of violence. Thinking back to these groups, I recall the frequent discussions regarding why self-assertion was difficult. Often the influence of upbringing was raised. Many of the participants described having been brought up in what I would characterize as MBG families. Stating their own views and asserting their wishes had always seemed to be a very difficult task for them unless they could feel certain that other people would give their approval. Somehow they had not been able to learn to either trust their own judgement or see their opinions as being as valuable as the next person's.

The balance between conformity and independence is always delicate. People who assert their own wishes and viewpoints and show no concern for those of others are likely to become terminally obnoxious. The risk for young people in MBG families, however, is that they will develop a nagging feeling of self-doubt and inadequacy that can remain with them long into their adult lives.

Permissive Style

THIS IS THE "LAISSEZ-FAIRE" STYLE. ACCEPT; DO NOT CHALlenge or criticize. Recognize that everyone is an individual with rights equal to your own. Do not impose your will on your children: you will crush their spirit. After all, do you want to raise and nurture a human being or create a robot? (By the time my first child became an adolescent, a robot sounded pretty good to me.)

I have a particular interest in the permissive style, as it had a strong influence on my early years as a parent. I had been very much part of the beat/hippy/flower-child generation of the sixties. In many ways this subculture was therapeutic for me; it allowed me to channel my rebellious nature without being incarcerated. One of my strongly held beliefs at that time was that we should run countries through consensus rather than giving individuals the power to control us through governments. So when I became a parent I was bound and determined not to treat my children in an authoritarian manner. I was still a rebel at heart, with a dislike of traditional hierarchies. The idea of a family headed by parents was as distasteful to me as a country headed by an elite few. After a few years I became a single parent and was able to allow my philosophy full expression. Joanne and Tim began to call me by my first name and I placed them in an alternative, free school system. I did not impose limits or set rules. These were discussed with the goal of reaching consensus. My voice was only one of three.

I still have a photograph of Tim when he was four. My sister-in-law took it out of disbelief and in the knowledge that she could use it to cause me endless embarrassment in the future. It shows a boy who could be a candidate for a starring role in a Dickens movie. Most striking is his hair; Tim had no use for a comb and hairdressers were not his friends. I had no wish to force the issue, so his hair is matted to the point where it looks like a failed attempt at braiding. As for his outfit, he had chosen to wear his maple-leaf swim shorts over his jeans and I was not about to stifle his creativity. My wife-to-be stared in disbelief as he prepared to leave for nursery school. She had intended to take him that day; I could not understand why she quietly, but emphatically, refused to leave the house with him.

I was a firm believer in self-expression. If Joanne threw something, I was understanding. "She needs to express her anger," I would state calmly to myself as I swept up the pieces. If she swore I knew it was because she had to release her feelings; this was much healthier than keeping it all inside and developing ulcers. Meanwhile Kathy (who was beginning to doubt that she was my wife-to-be) shook her head and began totally revising her view of mental-health professionals.

The permissive style of parenting lives on, although it has different faces. It no longer tends to be part of a rebellious subculture. In one form it is far more child-focused than it is a reflection of any general attitudes towards society. The parents' intentions are excellent; they value individuality and self-expression as much as I did—and, I hope, still do. They truly understand the enormous potential of children to develop, achieve, and create. To help develop this potential they often spend a great deal of time with their children. If a child seems interested in a particular activity, this is encouraged. The parents facilitate rather than direct. They provide opportunities; they rarely insist. The child's opinions are also given considerable weight. There is much encouragement to express views and feelings and there is the belief that children's potential includes the ability to make good and rational decisions.

As I am writing I am reminded of my continuing belief in certain aspects of this type of permissiveness. I share the view that if we offer appropriate opportunities, our children's interests and potential will usually develop in healthy ways. But this approach to child-rearing can lead to conflict. This tends to arise when the child becomes more involved with groups outside the immediate family—for example, when he begins attending nursery or elementary school. In most educational systems there are clear expectations for conformity. A wide variety of activities is available, but most are not seen as optional. There are lessons; there are times to do math, and there are other times to write in your journal. There are also prescribed ways of carrying out these activities. The parents' dilemma is how to balance their belief in the importance of individuality and self-expression with the growing demands that their children conform and learn to fit in with the group. The fear behind this dilemma is that conformity will stunt growth and that the price to be paid for becoming a member of the group will be both loss of self-reliance and suppression of their child's unique potential. As long as the dilemma remains unresolved, the child can find himself becoming more and more in conflict with others.

A second form of permissiveness has more to do with the parents' abilities than their attitudes. The permissiveness is by default; it is not an approach chosen by the parents, but is one that develops because they are unable to exert sufficient control. Sometimes adults who are extremely confident and capable in many areas of their lives find they simply do not know much about discipline. Attempts may be made to impose limits, but these often end in the parents' backing down in the face of the child's defiance. If the parent is victorious, this is only after a battle that leaves everyone feeling upset and angry.

The parents may be very loving and sensitive. Their love and sensitivity may, however, be working against them in some ways. One reason underlying their inability to exert control can be their unwillingness to act in ways that might cause the child to feel denied or disappointed. Children become aware of this "softness" quickly and have no difficulty learning how to melt their parents' hearts.

Whatever the underlying reasons, the parents are faced with the reality that they do not know how to assert their authority. They may complain bitterly about their children's behavior, and often with good cause. But they feel at a loss when addressing such questions as how to ensure that their child goes to bed before midnight or how to stop his using bad language or watching television for hours on end. A pediatrician in our community refers to some children as needing to be "bitted and bridled." Having a love of horses, I don't find this comparison between children and colts or fillies at all offensive. It also seems an accurate description of what needs to happen when permissiveness has led to the type of severe and recurrent conflict that can take most of the joy out of family life.

The impact of permissiveness on children has been studied for over thirty years. Permissive parents have been defined as those who, although often warm, make few attempts to control their children's behavior. They tend to impose relatively few demands or expectations and allow their children to regulate their own activities. Like the children from authoritarian families, those from permissive environments tend not to be self-reliant. In fact, the permissive style is likely to inhibit self-reliance even more than the authoritarian style. The hope may have been that, by not subjecting children to external controls and expectations, they will develop their own standards and will become confident in their own abilities. Apparently this is not so. An overly permissive home environment is more likely to leave children without either a clear sense of direction or the ability to trust their own decisions.

When describing children from permissive families, researchers have used the term "delayed socialization pattern." Part of this pattern is the lack of self-reliance I have just discussed. It also involves poor self-control and lack of social competence. There seems to be a real risk that giving children too much freedom will encourage them to develop into people who are self-centered and who show disregard for the feelings and rights of others.

The permissive style has an effect on the motivation to achieve. Children seem to need to have standards and objectives set for them. Later on they can take over responsibility for establishing their own goals, but they must first have the experience of working towards those provided by others.

I find it interesting that children themselves seem to be dissatisfied with the permissive style. I suspect most adolescents would be happy to tell you about how parents as a breed are too bossy and controlling, and they may believe that they would be much happier if they had a free rein when it came to managing their own lives. Research has indicated, however, that those who find themselves in this position are often far from being satisfied with the relationships they have with their parents.

Combining and Adapting Styles

QUITE OFTEN PSYCHOLOGISTS TRY TO SELL ONE parenting style and are heavily critical of the others. The democratic style is usually the chosen one and I will devote the whole of the next chapter to this approach. At the same time, I have a soft spot for elements of the other three styles. Being authoritarian has its merits, guilt is a wonderfully versatile and useful tool, and I owe some of the most exciting and memorable moments of my life to permissiveness. Elements of each style have their place. While we need to know how to discuss and negotiate matters with our adolescents, we also have to maintain the strength and determination to make firm rules when we believe our opinions and decisions should prevail. And guilt has a role in child-rearing. We want our teenagers to have a strong conscience; if they do not possess one by the time they reach adolescence, it is probably too late. I want my children to feel guilty when they are insensitive towards others and I want them to be critical of themselves when they are not striving to use their potential and talents. A permissive style will also be important at times. While I expect them to care about the opinions that I and others have of their behavior, I want them to have the ability to stand up for their beliefs in the face of opposition. Consequently, I have to give them the freedom to develop their own standards and values and not rely too heavily on others for approval and acceptance.

I have given up trying to get the balance exactly right. In fact, I now take some comfort in accepting that part of the condition of being a parent is to be permanently imbalanced. Even if I think I have developed just the right style as a parent, my children refuse not to grow up. Very quickly an approach that seemed to fit for the family will have to be overhauled as the children's needs and abilities change and develop.

Sometimes parents ask me if they will ever "get it right." My usual reply is, "I hope not." First of all, after twenty-five years of being a parent I haven't been able to get it right, so why should they? What's more, I'm the professional, so if there is a recipe for success I should get it first so I can sell it to them for an exorbitant fee. Finally, I believe all of us as parents have to ensure that we remain open to revising the way we deal with our teenagers. I see it as healthy to assume that there is always something that I can be doing a lot better. While research can give us rough guidelines and help us avoid some of the pitfalls, the manual for successful parenting does not exist and I doubt that it ever will.

FOUR

Can Families Be Democratic?

So Now We Hold Elections?

THERE IS ALWAYS A DANGER THAT PARENTS WILL EQUATE a democratic family with anarchy and loss of control. After all, one of the principles of democracy is "one person-one vote." Under this principle, holding on to a majority would mean that you could only have one child. Panic would set in if you gave birth to twins, with polygamy being the only way to restore the balance of power. Rather than adopt such fanciful solutions, I advocate the selective use of democratic principles. In other words, we (the parents) adopt only those principles that we think will be useful and ignore those we do not like. It sounds pretty authoritarian, but let's indulge ourselves.

Fifteen years ago I thought I believed in the "one person-one vote" principle, which, in effect, meant that everyone in the family had equal power. I'm not sure what finally led me to abandon this notion. Perhaps it was my growing awareness of the vulnerable position I was in as a single parent with two children. If Joanne and Tim could ever have agreed on anything, they would have had two votes to my one. Perhaps I also became more accepting of the fact that democratic societies need to have hierarchies; we choose people to have more power than the rest of us. Whatever the reason, one day I had a revelation. It was a thought that had instant appeal as a way of fending off the chaos I sensed developing in the family. I wanted us to remain a family in which power was shared. But, I reasoned, democracies have a prime minister or president. Someone has to occupy that position. Forget elections. I was obviously the most qualified and my children were promptly relegated to the back benches. Under our new constitution my term of office was somewhere in the region of twenty years.

Having established who the leaders are in the family, the task is to write the other guiding principles of the constitution. It is hard to select just a few of the principles of a democratic society that seem applicable, but there are some that are particularly relevant for families of teenagers.

Consultation and Communication

THE FIRST PRINCIPLE IS THAT PEOPLE HAVE THE RIGHT TO free speech and, in most instances, the right to be consulted when major decisions are going to be made. The government that doesn't listen to its citizens enough may well pay the price at the next elections. But since we have abandoned the idea of elections in families, the parents have the responsibility of ensuring that they invite opinions and feedback.

Whole books have been written about listening and communicating. I simply want to suggest to parents of adolescents that they take a careful look at the way communication takes place in the family. There are a number of questions I recommend parents ask of themselves. The first is: do you actively seek and invite your son's or daughter's opinions? Like many parents, I probably do not discuss matters in the family as much as I should. It is tempting to leave well enough alone when there do not seem to be any problems. Unfortunately, "leaving well enough alone" can all too easily become "letting things slide."

I see the job of a parent as being to create opportunities for ongoing discussion of the kinds of issues that so often create conflict, such as chores, bedtimes, curfews, school work, and restrictions regarding social activities. Sometimes families have a routine such as always having an open discussion during Sunday supper. For other families this may seem too formal. Whatever system is used, the question remains simple: do you ask for their opinions? You may feel this is unnecessary: parents often complain of being bombarded by their teenagers' opinions. But even if you feel you hear from them too much, bear with me and entertain the notion that you should nonetheless invite them to express their views. We all like it when our opinions are sought, even when there is no expectation that others will necessarily agree with us. What is important is feeling that our opinions are important and worthy of consideration. Teenagers are no different; in fact, I believe adolescents have a particularly strong need to feel that what they have to say matters too. They have spent so much of their lives listening to others at school and in the home. Asking for—as opposed to just getting—your teenager's opinions sends a clear message that you respect both her and her views.

The second question is: does communication tend to be primarily in response to a conflict or a crisis? It makes sense, of course, that issues are discussed when something is going wrong. A teenager's repeatedly coming home later than a specified curfew should not be ignored. Such incidents, however, are not usually the ideal starting points for discussion. So often they seem to lead to arguments in which no one is inclined to listen to the other person. A lot may be said and it is at these times that parents and teenagers complain of being bombarded by one another's opinions. The probability of any useful discussion, however, is low. After all, an offense has been committed. It is like arguing with a judge about a speeding ticket when you've been clocked at eighty in a fifty limit zone. You can try to make the case that the law should be changed and the judge might even agree with you, but you don't change laws in the courtroom.

While communication will inevitably be conflict-oriented at times, it should also be an integral part of family life. This is like the democratic process of reviewing matters through public hearings and debates in the legislative assemblies. Inviting discussion when no one is feeling angry or defensive increases the likelihood that family members can express their differing and sometimes opposing views without hurting one another.

The third question is: do you actually listen when the invitation to talk has been given? One of my toughest jobs as a family counselor is asking parents to be quiet in ways that are neither rude nor put me in danger of being seen as siding with the teenager. I can remember one father and his son Rob, whom I met with over the course of several months, primarily because of conflicts regarding school work. Although I never asked him, Rob's father must have won countless awards for public speaking and debating. He was intelligent, articulate, and humorous. He expressed his views in a well-organized way and always provided ample justification for his opinions. Rob was also bright and articulate, but he was no match for dad. Occasionally, his father would pause and ask him, "Well, what do you think?" I doubt if the reply was ever permitted to be longer than twenty seconds. It was usually terminated by the "Yes, I see what you mean, but ..." maneuver. (This is an excellent tactic. It halts the other person in his tracks by making him believe you might actually agree with him. It is followed, however, by a lengthy monologue in which you inform the person in no uncertain terms that you really meant "No, you're dead wrong.")

As I sat listening to the father I was struck by how right he was. Yes, Rob did have the potential to do better. If he spent less time on the telephone he would have more time to study. He could certainly benefit from a study skills program. He was in danger of unnecessarily limiting his options by not getting higher marks, and his father, who had led a varied, interesting, and largely successful life, was speaking from a position of greater wisdom and experience. But the more Rob had to listen and feel powerless in the face of his father's logic and well-reasoned arguments, the more I knew he was becoming quietly resentful and rebellious. His father had been winning the debates. Rob, however, was learning to fight back with his behavior. He knew as well as I did that his father could not make him work. Dad might control the debate, but Rob controlled his report card.

I wish I could now tell you of the brilliant intervention I made, with the result that father and son learned to communicate effectively and Rob went on to be a Rhodes scholar. It was not quite like that. I did help Rob talk about how hard it was to negotiate with his father. We developed the analogy of a face-off in hockey, with dad being in the NHL and Rob in Junior B. Both were accomplished players in their own right, but it was not exactly a fair contest. Dad did undertake to try to give Rob equal air time. He agreed he didn't need to use the "Yes, I see what you mean, but . . ." maneuver. Father and son also made a deal. Rob agreed to quit rolling his eyes and looking out the window when his father spoke. Dad agreed not to shake his head in immediate disagreement or smile in what he admitted was a somewhat condescending way when Rob expressed views that differed from his own. I doubt if the face-offs ever did become a fair contest and I have no idea what happened to Rob's marks, but it seemed their debates became more enjoyable and productive.

One family told me they had regular meetings at the supper table and used the ketchup-bottle method of ensuring everyone got to express their views. It is very simple. When the bottle is in front of you, everyone else has to listen. And there's no grabbing; when you want to speak, "Pass the ketchup please" is the way to go. I've never risked it. We use a squeezable bottle and I have visions of a free-for-all that could get very messy. But again, the method itself is relatively unimportant. What matters is that the family works out an agreement that all members—both teenagers and parents—have to listen as much as they talk. No one gets to be a star performer.

Negotiation and Power

LET US ASSUME THAT THE FAMILY HAS WORKED OUT A way of communicating that ensures everyone feels they have a voice that is listened to and respected. (Everyone also remains entitled to the occasional temper tantrum or irrational outburst, but these are kept to a minimum.) The next issue to be addressed is how much weight should be given to each person's viewpoint. I have argued that it is the feeling of being listened to that is important rather than whether or not other people agree with you. Yet, if I felt I never had an impact on what happens, I would soon begin to wonder why anybody bothered to ask me what I thought in the first place. In democracies people strive to balance the need for the government to have sufficient power to run the country with the right of each citizen to have input into the decision-making process. We all need to feel we have a measure of real power. As the everyday citizens in the family, teenagers also want real power. Sooner or later they are obviously going to get it, even if they have to wait until they are adults. The matter for parents to decide is how much power they should ask their adolescents to exercise and at what stage they should transfer this power.

It is probably the case that adolescents can assume greater responsibility than we recognize. The period of time between young children's dependence on parents to their independence as young adults goes by very quickly and it is hard for us to be aware always of how much they have grown. In Chapter Two I discussed the changes that take place in children's reasoning abilities as they enter adolescence. By the time children have passed the age of approximately twelve, they are usually able to do mentally what we often try to do for them. Parents may tell them at length about the likely consequences of their actions, but most adolescents are more than capable of this mental exercise. They can also work effectively with the abstract and hypothetical. Parents, particularly those with MBG traits, may encourage their teens to imagine how other people think and feel about certain situations. Adolescents can do this just fine; the term developmental psychologists use is "perspective taking," a skill that is well in place by the teenage years.

Having the abilities needed to make rational decisions does not, of course, guarantee that teenagers will. On the other hand, it's not a bad start. Like most skills, decision-making needs to be worked on. Sooner or later young people have to start practicing if they are to become proficient.

I favor a gradual and planned transfer of power, with emphasis on the word "planned." The idea is to avoid the development of conflicts in which teenagers are trying to win power while parents are staunchly defending their right to keep it. Often the hard part is deciding what areas of power can be transferred in this way. I suggest thinking in terms of three categories. The first is the "That's the way it is" category. It should be small and refer only to those situations in which you feel you will always have to insist on using the authoritarian style. Examples might be drug use, smoking in the house, attending school. In these areas the parents exercise their right to set limits that are not negotiable and trust that their adolescents will realize that this rigidity is a sign of caring.

The second category consists of the "Let's work it out together" group of issues. This is the largest of the categories and it requires both parents' and adolescents' learning how to negotiate. First of all, it has to be decided what issues are negotiable. Some examples come from a study in which teenagers were asked to identify the major areas of conflict with their parents. High on the list was the amount of time they were expected to be home, including always having to come home straight after school, having to eat supper with the family every evening, and always doing homework in their rooms. These issues are good candidates for the "Let's work it out together" category. Maybe some free time between the structure of the school day and the routine of family life is not so bad, and I doubt the wisdom of insisting that adolescents always eat supper with the family. Knowing that your son is alone in his room in the physical proximity of his books is absolutely no guarantee that any work is being done. I remember one girl I was seeing individually who, at fifteen, had decided to take a short mental "vacation" during the school year. As a result her marks fell dramatically. The parents were understandably most upset and in no time at all she realized that she had used up all her vacation time for many years to come. One new rule implemented was that she had to spend two and a half hours studying in her room every night. It was fascinating to listen to her describe the list of interesting things she could do in her room. Unfortunately, very few of the items on the list were even remotely connected to achieving at school.

Allowing negotiation of the rules about how much time teenagers spend at home often seems to be difficult for families. Perhaps one reason is that we find it hard to accept that, in some ways, the closeness and togetherness we enjoyed with our children when they were young cannot continue—at least, not in the same form. What made me decide that this issue had to be negotiated was the realization that, if I had to make strict rules to ensure togetherness, perhaps I was missing the point. It's like trying to make people have fun together or like one another.

Other issues that parents might consider for inclusion in the second category are chores and other responsibilities in the home, use of the family car, attending church, curfews, choice of friends, attendance at family gatherings, participation in family holidays, and choice of recreational activities. Please note that these are no more than suggestions for consideration. For instance, the religious beliefs and affiliations of some parents may not permit attendance at church to be negotiable. All I am recommending is that parents take the time to think about the many decisions they have typically made for their children and work on the assumption that most should be negotiable by the teenage years.

So what does negotiation actually involve? People who are bargaining in good faith want consensus: they want to be able to find a solution that is acceptable to all parties. To achieve this, they work hard to avoid conflict. If you invite your teenager's opinions regarding curfews, she needs to understand that you may have a different view and that she will have to listen to you as much as you will listen to her. As long as she discusses this matter with you, negotiation will continue. However, should she opt to engage in heavy eye-rolling, deep sighing, or verbal protests that exceed seventy decibels, the negotiations are over until she can treat you with the same respect you are willing to afford her.

Another critical part of negotiation is to be specific and concrete. Sometimes it is hard to stop negotiations developing into discussions and then arguments regarding general principles. Attendance at family gatherings is an issue that can illustrate this point. If, after thirty years or so as part of your own family, you are still getting together regularly, it says something about the strength of kinship. Your relatives may drive you to the brink of despair and insanity at times, but somehow they do offer a certain sense of security and continuity. Knowing that you probably drive them to the same brink also helps reaffirm your faith that the world can be just and fair. Teenagers, however, may not see it this way. For some, there may be an incentive, such as an interesting or attractive cousin. For others, watching the grass grow might be a more enticing proposition. If your teenager is one of the many who offer resistance to attending family functions, I give you the following challenge: taking into consideration all you know about your son's interests and preferences, try to come up with a more boring activity than the family get-togethers.

Be specific about your expectations. Does he have to attend all, some, or none of the gatherings? Assuming that the matter is negotiable, the answer has to be either "some" or "none." If the answer is "some," which ones do you want him to attend—every second or third, or just the ones on special occasions such as Christmas or Easter? As long as the negotiation focuses on specific issues such as these, there is plenty of room for discussion and compromise. The danger is that the parties will start arguing about principles and generalities. Parents may feel hurt and upset that their adolescents do not seem to place as much value on family as they do. This can initiate classic MBG lectures regarding how much Aunt Gladys will be hurt if he doesn't attend and how grateful he ought to feel because of all his grandparents have done for him. This will be countered by reminding you that all Aunt Gladys does is pinch his cheeks, ruffle his hair, and tell him to run along and play. And, while loving his grandparents dearly, Granddad insists on calling him Jimmy instead of Jim and Grandma never fails to bring out the family album to show him how much he looks like his dad when he was a boy. So the argument progresses with your espousing the virtues and importance of family involvement while he tries to get you to see how reunions offer a whole new dimension and meaning to the word "tedium." This type of conflict is never resolved. No one agrees and no solution is reached. The conflict surfaces time and time again. The opposing positions rarely change. Everyone knows what the other is going to say and no one is inclined to change or modify their standpoint.

All the issues that tend to lead to conflict can and probably should be reduced to specific questions. It is easier and more effective to discuss the time adolescents have to be home on school nights than to debate the value of an education or the relative importance of friends versus school. It is also likely to be more productive to discuss which specific jobs around the house will be a teenager's responsibility than to embark on the "You're part of the family too—don't you think you should contribute?" line of reasoning. I admit every once in a while I do not fight my urge to deliver such speeches, but I know that these momentary lapses will not help the negotiations and that sooner or later I must get back to trying to work out a specific plan and agreement.

Sometimes parents are concerned that making an item negotiable will be an invitation to conflict no matter how the issue is discussed. The expectation is that their own and their adolescent's opinions will be so far apart that compromise will be impossible and that they should, therefore, hold onto the responsibility for making the decision. I like to think of the development in organizational theory that has taken place recently. The previous models for business and similar organizations have been mainly hierarchical; for example, there is a president and a board of directors at the top, with power being exercised downwards through senior, middle, and junior levels of management. There has been a growing interest, however, in abandoning this hierarchy and establishing a weblike structure. In this structure there is a center of power, but decision-making is a responsibility that spreads out to the other parts of the web. The emphasis is on consultation and reaching consensus, and it seems that organizations using this approach can be very effective. From a more personal perspective, I have had the opportunity to be part of a number of committees and clinical teams over the years. Those headed by an autocrat who believes he or she has to make the major decisions to ensure that things get done only revive the rebellious side of my nature and make me want to argue, even if I might secretly agree. When the leader only asserts authority if absolutely necessary, I find myself enjoying being part of a group that, more often than not, willingly shares ideas and quickly moves towards finding a middle ground when opposing views are involved. My experiences with families have been similar. I have seen parents and teenagers who have remarkable capacity to fight with one another show equal capacity to reach a joint decision regarding rules and limits. Often I do no more than suggest how to proceed with negotiations and ask the family for permission to interrupt when it seems the discussion is getting too general and needs to be brought back to specific questions.

I believe the single most important step towards successful negotiating is to move away from the hierarchy and establish a climate in which everyone's opinion has weight. I have seen teenagers who are behaving in infuriating, aggressive, and immature ways in an effort to wrestle power and control from their parents show surprising ability to act responsibly when invited to share the power and control. I'm not maintaining that negotiation solves all conflicts and transforms families into clones of the Waltons or Brady Bunch. What can often be the case, however, is that a genuine transfer of power can strengthen rather than weaken the family unit. It can also help prepare teenagers for independence by providing them with the opportunity to develop their ability to make significant decisions and reach compromises.

The third category consists of areas in which you are willing to transfer all power. When considering items for the "It's up to you" category, it's tempting to relinquish responsibility for only those decisions that everyone knows are trivial. Being allowed to choose whether or not you will eat salad with supper or having the right to decide if you will wear your sneakers or boots may increase your teenager's range of responsibilities, but they are hardly giant steps towards emancipation.

I like to start from the position that almost all items in the "Let's work it out together" category should sooner or later be considered for transfer to the "It's up to you" group. Once again, I have in mind the fact that, as young adults who have just left home, they will probably be in living situations in which they will have to make all the major decisions themselves. When I think back to my experiences in the working world and remember the jobs I've had, I recall always appreciating the opportunity to gradually take on assignments and responsibilities. The "sink or swim" approach to personnel management lacks finesse and invites failure. Perhaps the same reasoning applies to preparing teenagers for adulthood. Gradually moving from the stage of shared control to one in which the teenager has most of the responsibility for her life can reduce the likelihood that she will go either completely wild or slowly to pieces when she is expected to be independent.

I can remember the joy and relief when we finally decided to let Tim manage his high-school career on his own. I have to admit that this decision was based partly on frustration; we never seemed able to get him to work as hard as we would have liked. But the decision also stemmed from the realization that, if he did go on to college or university, we were not planning to move into residence with him so that we could escort him to his classes. We had also decided that, if he chose to work rather than study after high school, we were not prepared to call every morning to see that he was up and was wearing clean clothes.

Of course, age and track record need to be considered carefully. Most parents could never see themselves allowing their thirteen-year-old son to stay home alone while they are away on vacation. Similarly, giving total responsibility for deciding when to come in at night would be unlikely to occur until the later teens. Demonstration of the ability to share this responsibility with parents effectively in the past would also be required.

I would like to touch on one area of anxiety that parents can have when it comes to allowing their adolescents to assume the major control over areas of their lives. The concern can be that their role as parents will be totally lost and that their children will be almost like boarders in the house who come, go, and do as they please. My recommendation, however, is that parents begin thinking about what it will be like to have an adult-to-adult rather than adult-to-child relationship with their offspring. Taking the example of activities outside the home, it can be useful to focus on how adults adapt and modify their behavior to accommodate one another. For example, my wife usually knows roughly where I am at all times. (This is no longer too difficult. The range of possibilities has become sadly narrower over the years. Excursions tend to be limited to the office, the after-hours medical clinic with the child whose turn it is to have the current family disease, and the supermarket.) I would like to believe that Kathy wants to know where I am and when I'll be back because she can't bear to be apart from me and that I occupy her thoughts during every waking moment. I have to concede, however, that maybe the reason she would worry if I were late and unaccounted for would be the panic that would set in at the prospect of having to cope single-handed with our children, her career, and my debts. So we exchange information about our respective schedules, not because we have to seek permission or approval, but because we care about each other. Teenagers have equal capacity for empathy. At times they may act as if they are indifferent to other people's feelings, but I do not believe giving adolescents power and control over their lives encourages insensitivity. To the contrary, increasing their responsibilities when they are ready to do so can encourage them to begin to behave towards you with the degree of consideration you voluntarily show in your relationships with other adults. The essential difference is that you ask, rather than insist. So you would probably request an approximate itinerary and ask your son to call if he is going to be home later than expected. A smattering of MBG may be necessary, but only to reinforce that you will worry about him just like you would worry if your spouse's whereabouts were unknown. A small but well-placed quantity of guilt adds strength to the fabric of any family.

We all know it takes time and consistent effort for adults to be able to live together. I see the final period before teenagers leave home as offering the opportunity to begin the process of learning to relate to them as adults. This period can become unnecessarily stressful when parents try to maintain the relationship strictly on a parent-child basis.

Crime and Punishment

DEMOCRACIES ALLOW CONSULTATION AND NEGOTIA-tion and they give real power to the people. Democratic societies also make laws and impose consequences for those who ignore and break the rules. In families this process is usually referred to as "discipline" and is another topic that has filled whole books. I will try to get away with three pages for two reasons. The first is that I cannot hope to outdo Barbara Coloroso, whose tapes about discipline and "natural consequences" are as helpful as they are entertaining. The second is that I believe many of the critical aspects of discipline have been covered in the previous sections on consultation and negotiation. If parents invite their teenagers to share the responsibility for decision-making, it is an easy matter to ask them to share the task of establishing consequences for not keeping to the rules they have helped make. You might assume that, if teenagers are allowed to decide on the punishment for their crimes, the most severe will be having to stay in their rooms between eight and nine on a Sunday morning. I will endeavor to persuade you otherwise. I mentioned that in my permissive days, I enrolled my first two children in a free school. This proved to be one of the more sensible decisions I made during this period of my life. The term "free school" is unfortunate. It conjures up images of teachers bound and gagged while the unruly masses finger-paint on the walls. To the contrary, the school provided an organized and regulated learning environment. The focal point was the daily school meeting in which students were given a large part of the responsibility for establishing rules and consequences. The role of the teachers was interesting. It was not typically to persuade the children of the need for discipline; rather, it was often to help them realize that being hung, drawn, and quartered was perhaps a bit of an overreaction to shoving a fellow student in the school yard. There was no messing with these youngsters. They knew that they were setting rules that applied as much to themselves as to others. That knowledge did not stop them from establishing consequences for misbehavior that were guaranteed to have a real and negative impact on the offender.

I have just come from a session with a mother and her sixteen-year-old son, Ben. Ben's mother never had to worry about discipline until two years ago. Prior to that, her son was a quiet and compliant lad who was a pleasure to live with. His mother also tended to be particularly lenient with him because of feeling that she needed to compensate for his father's leaving when he was a baby. When Ben stopped being compliant, he stopped in a hurry. By the time I began seeing them, he was on probation, had skipped school repeatedly, and seemed to have "fired" his mother as a parent. He is now in danger of being permanently evicted from the home and the tension in the family remains high. What struck me this evening, however, was his ability to negotiate rules and consequences. He wants to regain his mother's trust and knows that not skipping school is an essential condition. He successfully negotiated with her that, if he skips once, he will hand over his collection of hockey cards for a month. (Serious business I might add. He has five thousand cards, including one currently worth four hundred dollars.) Three incidents of skipping and he agreed that his mother gets to sell the collection and he will be given the money to pay for his room and board in another household. As a sign of good faith, Ben has offered to hand over his six Eric Lindross cards tonight. While the outcome of these negotiations is un-known, the intentions cannot be faulted.

While we all want freedom, I am convinced we have an equally strong desire for structure and controls. I start from the assumption that, if I invite my daughter to negotiate curfews, she will be fair and reasonable in helping to decide what the conse-quences will be for breaking the rules. The only point I would emphasize is to try and ensure that the consequences are logical, short-lived, and concrete. If she stays out later than agreed, having to sit at home next Friday evening helps repay the debt—and perhaps only one Friday night's internment is sufficient. Losing a right or privilege for months on end only encourages a sense of hopelessness that fosters resentment and rebellion rather than self-control. Not being allowed to go out also meets the criterion of concreteness. What tends to be a source of unnecessary frustration is to embark on lengthy discussions aimed at changing opinions, attitudes, or feelings. "Why did you agree to come in at twelve and not get back until one?" is about as logical a question as the judge asking, "Why were you driving at eighty in the fifty zone?" Unless you are an obstetrician on your way to a multiple delivery, your answer is irrelevant. You sinned and you have no defense. Your daughter was probably doing no more than living for the moment and having the type of fun and excitement you can only envy. At some point she may decide that giving in to impulse and whim isn't worth the hassle. Until then, be kind to yourself. Mete out the punishment with a minimum of words, lessen your chances of a stress-related illness, and trust that the general trend will be upwards.

Long-term Effects of Democratic Parenting

THE RESEARCH IS CLEAR. CHILDREN RAISED IN DEMO-cratic families tend to be more confident in their ideas and opinions. They have greater self-reliance and possess better decision-making skills. They are likely to view their parents as fair, while respecting their right to exercise authority. The studies suggest that parents who encourage their children to be independent, but still retain an interest in the young person's decisions, are most likely to produce autonomous, well-adjusted adolescents.

FIVE

Self-Esteem

What is Self-Esteem?

THERE HAS BEEN A GREAT DEAL OF RESEARCH INTO HOW people see themselves (self-concept) and how positively or negatively they evaluate what they see (self-esteem). What is evident is that our self-concepts are quite complex, and become more so as we develop. Not surprisingly, young children are relatively unsophisticated in the way they see and describe themselves. They also tend to be concrete and focus on physical characteristics or specific skills. For example, if an eight-year-old is asked to describe himself, a typical response will be: "I am tall and I have red hair. My friends call me 'Red' and I like that. I am on the baseball team and I want to be the pitcher. I love math. My parents work and we live in the country near a lake where I go fishing with my friends." By the time adolescence is well under way, the young person's self-concept has become more complex. Like most adults, adolescents begin evaluating themselves in terms of their beliefs, values, and personality characteristics. Certainly, more superficial characteristics, such as appearance, remain relevant and can be particularly sensitive issues in the teenage years. What is added to the self-concept, however, is the recognition of the importance of other dimensions. Part of a teenager's self-description, for example, might be: "I am an outgoing person and I try to be understanding with my friends. I worry about the environment and I want to become a biologist so I can help change things. I am usually fun to be with, but sometimes I just want people to leave me alone. I'm okay at school, but if I don't like the subject or the teacher I slack off." Such statements reflect the young person's capacity for self-awareness and insight. They also demonstrate the emergence of ideals and principles, and we know from research that these characteristics remain fairly stable over time; the values adolescents have tend to remain with them into adulthood.

Given that the self-concept becomes increasingly complex, it is not surprising that psychologists have had difficulty devising adequate measures. It now seems to be accepted that if you want to assess a person's self-esteem, you have to consider many different aspects of self-concept. Researchers have, for example, devised separate measures of how people evaluate their interpersonal skills (social self-esteem). I had a student who devoted her undergraduate thesis to developing a measure specifically of students' perceptions of their academic potential and skill. She demonstrated that academic self-esteem was quite distinct from other forms of self-evaluation. Overall, while there is lack of agreement regarding how many areas of self-concept are important, there seems to be no doubt that the number is high. One questionnaire devised for use with adolescents includes nine areas of self-concept, such as body image, educational attitudes and abilities, peer relationships, family relationships, and emotional characteristics.

In addition to specific areas of self-evaluation, there seems to be a more general aspect to how we see ourselves. This is often referred to as "self-worth." It is a basic belief that we are worthwhile and valuable as people. It is the ability to feel good about ourselves even when we are not being successful at what we are trying to do or are being criticized by others. I will be focusing on this type of self-esteem, which is probably the most critical for healthy development. The feeling of being acceptable as a person gives young people the confidence to develop relationships and take on new tasks and challenges. As parents we have an important role to play in helping our children see themselves positively. To grow up believing they are worthwhile and likeable people, children need to receive positive feedback from those around them and it is usually the opinions of their parents that carry the greatest weight.

Development of Self-Esteem

WE SEEM TO BE EXPERTS AT HELPING VERY YOUNG CHILDren develop a healthy self-image. This is fortunate, as our early experiences have a major impact on our subsequent development. With no effort at all, parents find cause to shower praise and approval on their infant children. In the first few hours after birth (when most babies look like they have been through the wringer) the new arrival is told how absolutely beautiful and wonderful she is. More accurate adjectives would be "wrinkled" and "squashed," but we all line up for the photo packages available on most maternity floors and prove yet again that beauty is truly in the eyes of the beholder.

Much of children's development is due to maturation. Humans are programmed to develop in a certain way and will do so provided they receive adequate physical care and live in a reasonably stimulating environment. This does not deter parents from treating inevitable changes as Olympian achievements. A baby will gurgle, grunt, and otherwise emit strange sounds and will be met with, "Who's the clever girl? You're trying to talk to me." Actually, she isn't trying to talk to you. She's just emitting gurgles, grunts, and otherwise strange noises. Language development comes later.

You could sell tickets for a baby's first steps if you could predict their occurrence. It's treated as an achievement akin to making the all-star hockey team and is an event waited for with keen anticipation. But it isn't really an achievement and there's not too much learning involved. Rather than being clever, the baby is simply doing what he has been programmed to do genetically.

And we continue to be liberal with our praise for toddlers. They return from play school with art work that defies identification. I am grateful to the staff who have written my children's names on a painting or drawing, as this is usually the only reliable method of determining which way up it should be hung. Having been told that they have made a picture just for you, what can you say but, "That's wonderful!" Inexperienced parents will follow this with, "What is it?" The more tactful or devious approach is, "Now come and sit down and tell me all about your picture." Having gathered enough information to determine that the seemingly random meanderings of the paintbrush represent a cow as opposed to a house or member of your family, the work is placed with ceremony on the front of the refrigerator.

I'm not suggesting we should stop lavishing praise on young children; they need our encouragement and approval in order to gain confidence in themselves. But somehow things change. The youngster who was so easy to applaud grows up and develops tastes, interests, and habits that are unlikely to evoke curtain calls. We encouraged them to listen to children's songs, but threaten to cut off stereo privileges if they persist in playing hard rock. We thought it cute and adorable when they paraded in dress-up clothes, but report chest pains at the sight of T-shirts proclaiming anarchy and rebellion. They never put away their clothes, they leave cups and dishes in their room; cleaning the bathroom sink is a behavior beyond their comprehension; they leave more dishes and cups in their room; you begin to believe that having homework is a figment of your imagination; and as yet more dishes and cups find their way upstairs, you give serious consideration to installing a dishwasher in the bedroom, except you'd never be able to get the door open wide enough. The number of issues that lead to frustration and conflict can grow steadily and a situation can develop in which disapproval and criticism overshadow praise and encouragement.

Balancing Criticism and Praise

THERE'S AN EXERCISE I'VE USED AT WORKSHOPS. I ONCE did it myself and found it quite informative. Each person gets two pieces of paper. You are asked to cast your mind back over the past week and, on the first piece of paper, write down as many examples as possible of comments you have made to your adolescent of a critical nature. You include even those gentle and subtle reminders that we give "for their own good." Examples would be: "You wouldn't have that cold if you had worn your woolly toque that Grandma knitted" (perhaps true, but neither would he have any friends) or "Jeffrey is such a nice boy, why don't you ask him over?" (this usually translates into "the friends you choose are bums or psychopaths"). I normally allow a good ten minutes for this part of the exercise.

I am sure you have guessed what the second part entails. The task is simply to list all those comments made of a positive nature, such as showing approval or giving praise. You don't need ten minutes for this. When I did the exercise I was already a practicing psychologist and my first reaction was to be somewhat appalled that the vast majority of feedback I gave my teenagers was of a critical nature. After all, I should have known better. But I had a second reaction. My defense mechanisms did not fail me. I reminded myself that if my teenagers would act in a more reasonable and civilized manner, I would happily be more forthcoming when it came to showing approval and gratitude. Nobody could expect me to give praise where it was not due or ignore the faults that were so evident in my offspring.

Unfortunately, the workshop leader was way ahead of me. Before I could even begin to present the case for my defense, she announced that she was sure that many of us would by now be trying to rationalize our critical tendencies. She asked us to go over our list of criticisms and decide how many were really necessary. She gave us some guidelines for deciding what constituted "necessary." If it involved safety, the item should stay on the list—for example, reprimanding your daughter for walking home alone late at night in a poorly lit neighborhood. An item would also be acceptable if it either provided new information or was likely to bring about a change in behavior.

It was hard to find items that qualified. I have yet to see a study that links toque-wearing with the common cold or other hazards. As for the "suggestion" about choice of friends, I assume that the son knows he could contact Jeffrey if he so chose. No new information here. I also assume that he knows only too well what you think of his friends and that the chances of changing his behavior are zero.

When I took a good look at my list of criticisms of my teenagers I had to admit that the vast majority were unnecessary, repetitious, and ineffectual. How many times did I need to tell Joanne that her marks would go up if she spent more time on her homework? It isn't exactly a novel idea. Anyone with two brain cells to rub together can figure that one out. But maybe if I kept reminding her of the relationship between homework and marks she would start working harder. Forget that. I've already given her the "Education is so important—you only get out of school what you put into it" lecture a hundred and sixty-seven times and how likely is it that the breakthrough will come on the hundred and sixty-eighth? And Tim did know the connection between going to school in a wrinkled T-shirt and his practice of throwing all his clothes in a pile on the bedroom floor. In fact, walking on his clothes was the closest I had ever seen him get to ironing.

Having convinced us that much of the negative feedback we gave our teenagers was both unnecessary and ineffectual, she turned to our second pages—not that there was much to turn to. I think there was consensus among us that we saw our teenagers as basically "good kids"—it just happened that they drove us crazy much of the time. But while we may have thought they were good kids we rarely seemed to take the opportunity to share this view with them. The task then was to think of examples of ways in which our teenagers had acted in the last week that we liked. I was able to recall that Joanne had helped with the yard work and had read a bedtime story to her little brother. Tim had been affectionate towards his baby sister. He had also been practicing his trumpet diligently for the Remembrance Day service, though listening to the last post while you are drifting off to sleep does make you wonder if you are going to wake up in the morning. And while it took effort and concentration, all of us were able to make respectable lists of actions that would warrant positive feedback.

I am not suggesting that we do tremendous damage to our teenagers by the negative feedback we give them, but we certainly don't help their self-esteem by so doing. In order to maintain a healthy balance between criticism and praise, our "basically good kids" need to hear that that is how we see them—and I'm not referring to the kind of mixed message that can run as follows: "We think you're a great kid, but . . ." Praise and approval should stand on their own and not be taken away as fast as they are given.

I am also not suggesting that we abandon opinions and expectations. We are obviously entitled to both. But what is often the case is that we spend a lot of time repeating ourselves in a way that is critical of our teenagers. They would call this nagging. Not surprisingly, when one group of researchers asked teenagers to list their complaints about their parents, nagging was easily the most frequent.

Lecturing is the more sophisticated form of nagging. I used to deliver many, so I find them easy to recognize when I meet with families. One parent usually starts and you are struck by how smoothly and eloquently he is speaking; practice and repetition lead to excellent delivery. The teenager for whom the lecture was written typically slumps in her chair adopting a posture of semi-sleep. While doing so, she emits a low groan or soft sigh and rolls her eyes. In some families it's a team effort. The parents take turns, reinforcing one another and presenting a formidable united front. The timing is precise. Each knows exactly when to take over from the other or provide comments to emphasize a point that has just been made.

I always find these situations awkward. The parents clearly want me to be the guest lecturer, perhaps in the hope that a trio of voices will succeed where the duet has not. There are two problems with this. The first is that it is extremely difficult—if not impossible—to work effectively as a family counselor if you take sides. The second is that I know I won't be any better at lecturing their offspring than I was at lecturing mine. If I am lucky, the teenager may listen to me with a facade of respect, but inwardly she will be slouching, sighing, and rolling her eyes, just as she did for her parents.

I have suggested to some families that they might want to make a tape. I recommend this in all sincerity, as the lecturing can become a source of much frustration. Usually there are a few key lectures that could readily be put onto audio cassettes. At the appropriate moment you simply hand the relevant tape to your son or daughter and tell them to go and listen to it in their room. Whether they play it or not is immaterial. They know exactly what it says anyway. I am not sure if anyone has actually made such a tape, but perhaps just the realization of how unnecessarily repetitious and critical we can allow ourselves to become as parents helps us change. A far better use of our time and energy would be to review the expectations and rules. Perhaps it is time that the issue we are lecturing on should become the teenager's responsibility with no, or very little, parental involvement. Perhaps not. If we decide that the issue is one that cannot be left just to our teenager's discretion, it may be the case that renegotiation of the expectations and rules is called for. In yet other situations we may be confident that the rules are fair. The job then is to impose consequences in a straightforward, matter-of-fact way. Imposing consequences is usually more than sufficient to register our disapproval. Prolonging the point only encourages unnecessary debate, and teenagers can find themselves defensively trying to justify their actions even when they truly know they are in the wrong.

There are two other approaches to restoring a balance between criticism and praise that I have found useful. The first involves not allowing our view of our children to be determined only by the present. When families seek counseling, it is, of course, because they are going through a period of particular difficulty and stress. Quite often parents are very angry at their children and are exasperated by their attitudes and behaviors. Rarely, however, has the situation at home always been this way. To the contrary, it is far more likely that the period in which there has been conflict is relatively small in comparison to the total amount of time the parents and children have been together. To help me gain a better understanding of the family, I sometimes spend a session playing "This is Your Life." I am a sucker for baby pictures and I really do not find other people's family albums boring. So I ask parents to bring these in and we look at them together. While I am learning about the family, the parents and teenagers have the opportunity to recall the closeness and positive feelings in their relationship that may have become masked by the recent disputes. I can remember a fourteen-year-old girl, Tina, and her mother who were engaged in a major struggle for power and control. At times it seemed they despised or even hated one another and I was becoming concerned that perhaps their relationship was irreparably damaged. The first time I heard them talk to each other, rather than argue, was when they recalled Tina's trying to pull her front teeth out after she had learned that, with the good services of the tooth fairy, these were as good as money in the bank. Tina also listened intently to her mother (a new behavior in our sessions) as she talked about what a cute and lovable baby she had been. I wanted to know if the closeness had been there, and I believe they needed to be reminded that it had. They agreed that, in a very real sense, they missed one another. The arguments certainly continued, but perhaps reaffirming that they both cared about one another and wanted to become closer again made the conflicts less destructive.

A second approach to restoring the balance is to try to become aware of the important, but sometimes hidden ways in which teenagers have developed. When discussing the definition of self-esteem I referred to how attitudes and values become a significant part of adolescents' descriptions of themselves. Sometimes we tend to assume that their beliefs and interests are impulsive and are likely to be short-lived. In some regards this may be true. It is also the case, however, that adolescence sees the emergence of values that often prove to be stable. For example, issues such as individual freedom, social responsibility, and establishing a society that is just and tolerant become important for many adolescents. Social scientists who have studied the development and shifts in values have noted that teenagers are often concerned with matters such as social and economic discrimination, racial prejudice, and pollution. In fact, they seem to be more involved in such issues than previous generations and their attitudes reflect a high level of tolerance and flexibility.

It can be hard to be aware of the deeper aspects of your teenager's development when you are confronted with a son who does not seem capable of taking responsibility for simple things, such as cleaning the kitchen counter after making a sandwich or putting his clothes in the laundry hamper. Having to deal with these surface, but exasperating behaviors can create a smoke-screen that prevents our seeing aspects of our children's personalities that we would probably applaud.

I have a particularly fond memory of a fourteen-year-old client, Michelle. The family came to see me because of the rapid and disturbing changes in her behavior. Michelle began wearing nothing but dark clothing; she listened to heavy-metal music; she had experimented with alcohol and possibly soft drugs; and she was becoming openly defiant towards her parents. The parents were very concerned about her moral development; they had reached the point where they felt all their efforts to instill healthy values in their daughter had failed. This feeling of failure was becoming very damaging. They were beginning to see Michelle as bad and hopeless; she, in turn, saw her parents as no longer liking or respecting her. After spending some time talking with Michelle alone, I found I had a different view of her. Yes, her behaviors were troubling, but it was also my impression that the parents had been successful in raising a daughter who had some very fine principles and standards. I recall reading her poems. Some of these expressed her hopes for world peace; others talked of the difficulty she was having reconciling her family's upper-middle-class lifestyle with her growing realization that so many of the world's population had to contend with lifelong deprivation and hardship. I was struck by how articulate and perceptive she was when discussing her views regarding religion and politics and, in some ways, she made me aware of my own shortcomings. She was expressing a degree of concern about the state of the world that I had shared passionately as an adolescent. Like many of my generation, however, my social conscience eventually seemed to be taking a back seat to more self-serving goals, such as my career.

The reasons to be worried about Michelle's behavior remained, but there also remained reasons to be proud of her. For the parents, the belief that they had lost their daughter was generating strong feelings of self-reproach, anger, despair, and pessimism. My goal became that of presenting Michelle to them in a different light—as someone whose behavior certainly needed to be brought under greater control, but whose underlying personality was sound and healthy in many respects. The behavior problems could then be seen as warranting intervention without their causing the severe damage to relationships that could result in the parents' losing respect for her.

One way in which I became more aware of the depth and quality of my own teenagers' personalities was through reading some of their essays and papers. I was occasionally permitted to read these, as long as it was understood that my role was not that of critic. It was interesting to hear their thoughts and analysis of human behavior arising from books such as *Lord of the Flies* or to become aware that they had the ability to wrestle with complex issues such as capital punishment, racial discrimination, and sexual equality. I also learned to take the opportunity to ask them more about their views and opinions on topics that were current, such as abortion and the military offensive in the Middle East. Listening to them talk, debate, or argue was stimulating and enjoyable; it also reinforced my respect for them as people. They still rarely cleaned the counter after making a sandwich and the laundry hamper remained conspicuously empty, but I was glad that their thinking could be infinitely more mature than their behavior seemed to be at times.

The Gift of Time

I CAN'T REMEMBER WHEN I HEARD THE COMMENT THAT the greatest gift you can give your children is your time. I can remember sitting in my office with a fifteen-year-old boy, John, who was in tears as he recalled his seventh birthday. His father had promised to take him skating—just the two of them. When the day came his father told him they would not be able to go as he had to visit a friend. The memory of this event continued to have as much impact as it had eight years previously because it had been reinforced by a number of similar incidents throughout the course of his childhood. Sadly, John had come to see himself as someone who ranked low on his father's list of priorities.

There are always songs that have a strong impact on you whenever you hear them. "Cat's in the Cradle" is one that I always listen to intently whenever it is aired. It talks of a father who never seemed to have enough time for his son. You are not given the impression that he did not love his son; it just seemed that other things got in the way. He was busy building a career and this takes a lot of time. There would always be another day to play ball. But somehow there wasn't. His son grew up and moved away. His father eventually found himself wanting to spend more time with his son. Maybe he was hoping to enjoy a closeness that they had never achieved. But it proved to be too late; his son had his own life in which his father could not play a major part.

It seemed that the song could have been written about John and his father. The difference was that John was making it clear that he wanted things to be different. Rather than becoming defensive, his father was open to taking a careful look at their relationship. It surprised him that he was so important to John; it pleased him as well. I quickly became redundant. They knew what the problem was and they were more than capable of fixing it themselves.

Perhaps our time is the greatest gift we offer our children because it is a clear statement regarding how important and worthwhile they are. If you choose to be with someone, you are letting them know that they matter to you and that you like their company. After all, if I were confronted with people crossing the street whenever they saw me coming, my self-esteem would take a severe battering.

I have often talked with parents who are at a loss to know how to spend time with their teenagers. They no longer want you to read to them or play another game of "fish." You could go to the movies together, but chances are you would never agree on what to see. You could talk about your day, although this may cause your son or daughter to experience heights of disinterest and boredom that exceed their wildest dreams.

My daughter taught me that being together can be an extremely simple matter. Joanne once remarked that she liked it when I was at home. This surprised me greatly. Joanne's communication at that time consisted primarily of rolling her eyes, banging doors, and heavy sighing (I can still hear those sighs after all these years). I had reached the opinion that, to her, my presence was as welcome as acne. Then, out of the blue, she remarked that I was away from home a lot and said it in a way that communicated her disapproval. What I came to realize was that she liked my being around. Sometimes we might sit in the same room; on rare occasions we even talked. At other times she seemed to ignore me completely and I had to work hard to convince myself that my being in the house mattered to her at all.

Over the course of the years with my children I have also learned that there are specific activities that we can enjoy sharing. I believe that there is usually a common ground between parents and teenagers, although it may be far from being a vast expanse. There is often at least one television program that could be watched together, and junk food (in moderation, of course) can make the event special. Now that I think of it, many of the activities I share with my children center on food and sedentary activity (I know my strengths). For the more adventurous, the North American passion for sports can often provide the link between the generations.

I will not attempt to provide a comprehensive list of what the common ground can be. Once families have set their collective minds to the task, they can be quite creative in thinking of ways in which they might enjoy being together. Quite often the obstacle to their doing this has been the assumption on both sides that neither is interested.

I am also convinced of the value of spending time with one's children individually. For those of us who have been blessed with more than one teenager at the same time, the difference between our children when they are together and apart can be dramatic. You may have been more fortunate, but as far as I am concerned, the term "sibling rivalry" could have been invented for my first two. Joanne and Tim had an unbelievable capacity for conflict. If one had offered an innocent "good morning," the other would have immediately responded with a meteorological challenge and off they would go. Squabbling seemed to be their major form of entertainment. (It was during this period that the title of this book came to mind.) Being with them individually was a very different experience. They seemed to be so much older. At weaker moments I even suspected they were rational human beings.

Our lives can be very demanding. Families with two working parents are rapidly becoming the norm. We often encourage our children to be involved in outside activities, with the result that there is little time left for us to be together. Yet somehow we still need to make sharing time with our children a regular part of family life. They need to know that, whatever other demands are placed on our time, we value their company.

SIX

Sexuality

Did I Miss the Sexual Revolution?

AS A TEENAGER I WAS LED TO BELIEVE THAT I WAS IN THE middle of a sexual revolution. I kept wanting to ask where it was being held, but I never had the courage. In the eighties I heard the revolution was over and I was left feeling that I had forever missed the chance to be part of history-in-the-making.

But did the revolution really happen? The answer seems to be yes and no. It depends on what area of sexuality is being studied. It does seem that attitudes have changed; for example, there is greater acceptance of premarital sex now than was the case in the fifties. The notion that premarital sex is more acceptable for males than females is also less popular. This double standard has been extremely strong and rigid in the past.

Changes in attitudes do not necessarily mean changes in

behavior. Are adolescents more liberal or permissive when it comes to actually engaging in sexual behavior? This is not an easy question to answer accurately. First of all, how can you be sure that adolescents (or adults) will answer questions regarding their sex lives truthfully? For example, when premarital sex tended to be frowned upon, adolescents might not want to admit to any experience with intercourse. When the social climate changed, perhaps they then felt reluctant to reveal their virginity. And that's only the start of the problems. You have to be sure adolescents know what you're asking. One researcher found that teenagers do not always understand common terms; one of the definitions given for losing virginity was "masturbating to a climax." Another teenager thought sexual intercourse was no more than socializing with the opposite sex.

It is also hard to do truly representative research: findings that relate to black college students in New York do not necessarily apply to white employed high-school graduates in Alberta.

So, what do we know? It seems safe to conclude that premarital sexual intercourse is more prevalent today than it was a generation ago, as are both "light" and "heavy" petting. Most of the increase, however, appears to result from the declining influence of the double standard. In the fifties and sixties less than one-third of girls had intercourse before the age of nineteen; now over half are sexually active with boyfriends. For the boys it seems that the statistic has remained fairly constant at around 70 percent, although some researchers feel a slight increase may have occurred.

Masturbation is the most common form of sexual expression among adolescents. By far the majority of teenage boys and girls masturbate; the estimate for boys often exceeds 90 percent. And it seems that the practice has been immensely popular for as long as people have conducted surveys. The attitudes towards it, however, have changed. While the topic is still one that teenagers find confusing and sometimes worrying, the extreme guilt and fear that used to be associated with masturbation have largely disappeared. I will return to this topic later in the chapter, as it provides an illustration of how myths and outrageous assumptions helped create anxiety about sex.

We are far from understanding what determines sexual preferences. It used to be thought that it was the way in which a child was raised that determined if she or he would be homosexual. More recently, evidence has come to light that biological/genetic factors may have an important influence. Whatever the reasons, sexual preferences are probably well on their way to being established by the time children enter the teenage years. This underlying preference needs to be distinguished from the sexual experimentation with the same sex that can occur in adolescence. For example, over one-third of boys report at least one voluntary homosexual activity that progresses to the point of orgasm. By the time they are entering adulthood, however, over 90 percent of adolescents will have an exclusively heterosexual orientation. This percentage has probably remained the same over the past fifty years.

So in some ways there has been a "revolution," but it is probably less dramatic than many of us think. Adolescents themselves typically overestimate how sexually active their generation has become. For example, if you ask teenagers what they believe *other* teenagers are doing, you will soon be believing that virgins are an endangered species. And you have to be careful when it comes to the statistics. While they can be very useful in helping us understand behavioral trends, they can be misleading if used too selectively. For example, if I took the statistics for nineteen-year-old girls over the past few decades I could proclaim, "Researchers Find a 200 Percent Increase in Teenage Sex." Now that's revolutionary talk. I could also justify the headline, "Most Seventeen-Year-Old Girls are Virgins—and They're Still Happy."

Are We Smarter about Sex?
A Look At History

WHEN PEOPLE TALK ABOUT THE SEXUAL REVOLUTION, they are typically referring to the changes in behavior and attitudes they believe have occurred in the last few decades. But what about knowledge? Do young people have a better understanding of sexuality? Do they have the information and facts that are needed whenever we are trying to make rational decisions about important areas of our lives? And how much information should they get? If you tell them too much, will you encourage them to be sexually active? Who should teach them about sex?

Our stage in history is often referred to as the "information age." Sexuality, however, is notably absent from the list of subjects in which most young people are well-versed. It continues to be a topic that many find embarrassing and so they don't ask questions or discuss their fears openly. I do not believe this is because sex is so personal a topic that it cannot help but be somewhat embarrassing. There are cultures in which our taboos about sex simply do not exist and in which the topic is dealt with in a relaxed and open manner. But we had the Victorians. While their era may have brought about many exciting and positive changes in society, they left us with a legacy of myths and anxieties regarding sexuality that we have yet to bury. This was the generation that advised people to cover table legs for fear of arousing men's passions. Not surprisingly, if table legs were such a hot topic, any more obvious form of sexual arousal or expression had to be a major cause for concern. As an illustration, I want to discuss the most widely practiced sexual behavior and one that received a lot of attention from the Victorians.

There is something about the topic of masturbation that promotes a rapid departure from reason and common sense. One of the more enjoyable experiences of my graduate student days was preparing a paper on the history of sexuality. It never ceased to amaze and interest me how so many educated and respected people could have held such outrageous beliefs. Let me introduce you to Dr. Kellogg. His book *Plain Facts About Sexual Life* was published just over a century ago. He devoted a large section of the book to the topic of the "secret vice" and proclaimed that "this sin is one of the most destructive evils ever practiced by fallen man."

Having got the attention of his audience, he proceeded to list the symptoms of the secret vice. Telltale signs included stooped posture, eating clay pencils, a taste for spices, and suspicious positions in bed (he left it to our imaginations to determine what these might be). Not eating clay pencils wouldn't be too much of a sacrifice, but having to choose between no cinnamon on your French toast and being seen as a sexual deviant was a bit much.

That's not the half of it. Adolescents suspected of masturbating were forcefully discouraged from continuing the practice. One technique was to place a spiked ring around the penis; an erection under these conditions was far from pleasurable. Another was to attach a device to the penis that activated an alarm if an erection occurred. This brings a totally new dimension to the image of bells ringing at the height of sexual passion. In the light of today's knowledge, these interventions were absurd. Many years ago I published a number of papers in the area of nocturnal erections. While I hasten to add that there was a legitimate reason for this research, I just want to make the point that all normal males spend approximately one-third of sleep with a partial or full erection that has nothing to do with being sexually aroused. So imagine the impact when the local general store got its supply of spikes and alarm systems. By midnight the noise in the neighborhood would have been deafening.

Girls were not exempt. The bicycle, for example, became popular in Kellogg's time. This was not the innocent invention you might have assumed it to be. Bicycles require pedalling and involve sitting on saddles. A Dr. Libby Muncie-Smith counseled parents regarding the implications of bicycle riding for their daughters. She suggested that mothers have their daughters ride their bicycles naked. The purpose was to ensure that the action of pedalling did not bring the genital area and the saddle into a meaningful relationship. Again, I am the victim of an overactive imagination. Where did these inspections take place? Hardly in the front parlor. On Christmas morning was there really a procession of modern-day Lady Godivas parading down Main Street in front of their concerned parents?

I cannot leave this subject without going back to Dr. Kellogg, whose name probably sounds familiar to you. His family entered the food business. Dismayed by adolescent tastes for spices and other additives, they set out to produce a breakfast cereal that would embody self-restraint and at least ensure that the start of the day had a flavor of purity. Cornflakes have continued to cool teenage jets for over a century.

Was all this thinking ridiculous? It is possible I am being too critical; after all, we all get smarter with hindsight. In my defense, I note that prominent writers of the time usually made two claims. The first was that masturbation caused very serious problems, ranging from tuberculosis to insanity. Pictures resembling wanted posters were even published portraying victims of masturbation with glazed eyes , drivelling saliva from the sides of their mouths. The second claim was that masturbation was a common problem. If you put these two claims together, the obvious conclusion would be that every time you stepped out of your front door you would be surrounded by drooling zombies. While there may be times when all of us feel we are surrounded by idiots we quickly recover a more balanced view of the human race.

People now make jokes about masturbation causing insanity or hair growth on the palms of hands. The recent books on sexuality designed for adolescents will echo this humor. I have not encountered one that condemns the practice; typically they emphasize that masturbation, itself, does not cause any psychological or physical damage. Yet somehow the high level of fear and anxiety that was so much part of Victorian thinking persists. If you ask teenagers what topics concerning sex they find confusing and would like to know more about, masturbation is high on the list. It is also a subject they find particularly embarrassing to talk about— more so than others, like petting or even intercourse.

The anxiety and embarrassment that continue to accompany the general area of sexuality in our society present some obstacles and pitfalls for adolescents. After all, the more embarrassing a subject is, the more people will want to avoid dealing with it openly. But sexuality doesn't simply go away: hormones can't be ignored and the psychological changes in puberty stimulate the sex drive no matter how many cold showers are taken. So teenagers will inevitably try to understand sexuality, but will often not seek information from reliable sources. I have occasion in my practice to talk to both adults and young people about their sexual histories and often ask how they obtained information about sex when they were growing up. Almost always their teachers were their friends and the schoolyard was the classroom. It is a law of nature that the less people know about a subject, the more they will speculate and theorize and eventually begin believing they have discovered the truth. Psychology is living proof of this law. Thus I continue to meet otherwise intelligent young people who have the strangest beliefs about sex and who are trying very hard, but unsuccessfully, to make sense of the rumors, stories, and "facts" they have heard.

In the absence of reasoned, well-balanced sex education, it is difficult for our teenagers to make sensible decisions. While schools have taken a strong role in providing this education, parents can be an important source of information and understanding. In this respect, I believe we can make a valid contribution to a necessary part of the sexual revolution.

Go Ask Your Father

I GREW UP IN AN ERA WHEN MOST FAMILIES AVOIDED THE topic of sex. Mine was no exception. Like so many of my peers I was given a book, and some thirty years later I am still wondering how it mysteriously appeared on my dresser. Most of it was boring; a description of eggs going down tubes did not excite me in those days. I distinctly recall being bitterly disappointed at the absence of pictures, and the advice it gave me was far from acceptable. Its prescriptions included vigorous sports, the standard cold showers, and no chocolate. In my capacity as the neighborhood slug who viewed walking to the candy store as a workout, it was hard to develop rapport with the author.

Have things changed much? Probably not as much as we would like to believe. Every so often a survey is conducted that confirms that parents are way down on the list of sources of information regarding sex. The same type of survey tells us that teenagers want more information and that they would not mind hearing it from us. The topics they would like on the curriculum include sex drive, homosexuality, masturbation, premarital sexual ethics, orgasm, and birth control.

I have to confess that I was not very good at teaching my first two children about sex. The paradox was that I was very comfortable talking to couples and young people about the intimate details of their sex lives during my professional life. At home it was a different story and I conned myself into believing that my silence was justified on the grounds that I was protecting their innocence.

I intend to take a very different approach with my other offspring in the belief that sex education in the home protects children rather than exposes them to risks. We now know that adolescents who receive sex education from their parents are, in fact, somewhat more conservative and responsible regarding sexuality than those who do not. They are less likely to become involved in premarital sexual intercourse, and those girls who do become sexually active are less likely to have an unwanted pregnancy. In general it seems that sex education in the home or school simply does not lead to the permissiveness that many people feared would follow the "loss of innocence."

Adolescents need two types of information. The first is factual and the second is more to do with attitudes, values, and feelings. When it comes to facts, don't hesitate to refer to books, as well as the videos that are becoming increasingly available. I hasten to add that these should not suddenly appear on your son's or daughter's dresser; this only communicates the idea that his or her emerging sexuality is something to be embarrassed or ashamed about. Parents should always review the material first—both as a refresher course for themselves and to ensure that the information is clear and acceptable to them given their religious and moral viewpoints.

There are many excellent books and videos today that discuss such topics as sexual arousal, erections, menstruation, wet dreams, pimples, masturbation, sexual orientation, differences in breast development, birth control, and sexually transmitted diseases. Some offer humor as well as information. One of my favorites is the book *What's Happening To Me?* The cartoon picture of a boy on a diving board looking at two girls and being confronted with a bulge in his swim shorts says it all when it comes to reassuring boys that they are not alone if they have found themselves with an unwanted erection.

Some parents find that the structure of reading a book or watching a video together helps overcome the awkwardness they feel when trying to discuss sex with their children. Quite often it is the same-sex parent that takes on this role, but there are no hard-and-fast rules about this matter. Being a woman will give a mother an edge when it comes to relating to her daughter's sexuality and the same obviously applies to fathers and sons. From another perspective, however, being with the opposite-sex parent can reinforce the idea that sexuality can be an open, rather than taboo, subject in the family.

One of the topics about which teenagers tell us they would like to be better informed deserves special mention. The term "safe sex" is heard frequently these days and is perhaps one of the most important matters for parents to address with their adolescents. The consequences of becoming sexually active can be extremely negative; the most obvious example is AIDS, which has become the deadliest of the sexually transmitted diseases. And each year over one million babies are born in North America as the result of unwanted pregnancies among teenagers. Most of the mothers will keep their babies, and while single teenagers can be excellent parents, many find the task overwhelming and their children suffer as a result. Some will marry because of becoming pregnant, but the likelihood of divorce is very high among this group. Some 40 percent of teenage pregnancies will be terminated by voluntary abortion. For a number of girls this may be experienced as a welcome relief from the stress of pregnancy, but for others it can lead to feelings of guilt and self-reproach they find hard to overcome.

The research referred to earlier reassures us that giving our children information regarding safe sex helps them make responsible decisions rather than encouraging them to be sexually active. So give them the straight goods. Remember that almost one-third of younger adolescents believe they cannot get pregnant unless they want to. Others believe there are truly safe times during the menstrual cycle (there aren't) or that the withdrawal method guarantees they won't get pregnant (it doesn't).

It is important to add that using scare tactics when discussing safe sex is probably not a good idea. As parents, it is hard not to be afraid for our teenagers. For example, although the likelihood of contracting AIDS is very low in the general population, we cannot conclude that it simply could not happen to our son or daughter. But social psychologists have long known that if you make people too anxious, they may block out your message. It is likely to be more effective if parents present the information, discuss the risks, and voice their concerns in a relaxed, matter-of-fact manner.

While information regarding safe sex, masturbation, and many other topics is important to provide, so is a forum for exploring attitudes and values. I usually find it encouraging when I talk to teenagers about how they make decisions regarding sexual relationships. Whether or not they are sexually active, they typically emphasize issues such as commitment, caring, and respect when they talk about relationships. They may be concerned about pressure to become more sexually active, but the motivation to resist this pressure is often stronger than the desire to conform to other people's expectations.

In my view it can be helpful for even preadolescents to be involved in discussions with their parents regarding how they will make decisions about sex. Invite them to give you their opinions about when a relationship should include sexual intimacy. Share yours. If you differ, encourage a debate and resist the temptation to lecture that plagues most of us. Ask how young people these days resist pressure. Talk about how you dealt with this issue. This can lead to a discussion of gender differences. As much as I hate to admit it, the male of our species has historically had more difficulty when it comes to handling sexual urges. I should add, however, that it seems that teenage boys these days place more emphasis on sex being just one part of a relationship than was the case in previous generations. Still, we probably have a long way to go, and a daughter needs to know that she does not have to assume any responsibility for her boyfriend's becoming overly aroused. If he complains of an ache, she might want to offer a sympathetic sigh, but an icy stare that communicates callous indifference will do just fine.

Fathers can have a particularly strong impact on their sons when dealing with the issue of sexual rights and responsibilities. Date rape is far more common than we once believed. A discussion of how we, as men, are more likely than our partners to allow sexual passion to become sexual aggression can be very productive. It is to be hoped that fathers can relate this topic to what has been modeled for years in the home—namely, that power has been shared between the parents without either exercising control through flexing muscles and intimidation.

When adolescents are asked about sexual ethics and morality, they typically stress their right to make their own decisions. There may be times when we need to be very directive and impose limits so as to protect our children from situations we know can be very damaging to them. For the most part, however, I believe our role is to act primarily as consultants to our teenagers. By offering information, encouraging debate, and sharing our own experiences and opinions, we can both respect their right to form their own moral standards and have a positive influence on decisions they do make.

Be Home by Ten:
The Chaperon Needs Her Sleep

BY NOW I'M SURE SOME OF YOU WILL HAVE HAD ENOUGH of this general discussion and will want an answer to the question: "My daughter wants to date and she's not yet thirty-five; what should I do?"

Some families have very definite guidelines. I remember talking to a boy who knew he wouldn't be allowed to date until he was sixteen. Michael was fourteen at the time. He was a delightful lad and I know he'll become an incurable romantic. He offered no argument with the rule; in fact, he seemed to be capitalizing on it by using the time to plan his first date in great detail and savor the delights of anticipation. The date was scheduled for the evening of his sixteenth birthday. Michael knew where they would go and what they would do. He had rehearsed possible conversations and planned activities that would keep them occupied should there be any awkward moments. I could have kicked myself when I made the completely unnecessary and mundane point that the plan would only work if he actually had managed to find someone to go out with him. I felt the guilt deserved by people who burst balloons and rain on parades and for the next few weeks nothing was said about the topic. Then Michael returned triumphantly with the news that a girl in his class, who was sure she had nothing else booked that day, had promised to be his date. Although I never learned if the big day materialized, I am sure the fantasy sustained him till he turned sixteen.

But should a parent set such an arbitrary limit? This is a question I am asked periodically and it's hard to answer. As a parent I've never felt the need to set such a limit. Our oldest children didn't seem particularly interested in dating in their early teens. In fact, we were beginning to feel that the only way we'd get them off our hands was to arrange marriages for them. Speaking as a psychologist, I always stay where I believe all counselors and therapists should be when it comes to matters of this nature—on the fence. What I will do, however, is discuss a number of issues related to dating that I think are worth considering.

First of all, what is dating? This may seem an unnecessary question, but the pattern of girlfriend-boyfriend relationships has changed over the past few decades. There is less emphasis on the formal date and more on spending time together in a group that includes both sexes. Teenagers tend to have a number of opposite-sex friends and they may socialize periodically as a couple without dating as boyfriend and girlfriend. The statement, "But he's just a friend" is less likely to be a cover for a secret romance than it was in my generation. Given this pattern of relationships between the sexes, establishing rules can be more difficult. Will your son be permitted to socialize with a female friend as a couple provided it remain strictly platonic? At what point do you consider them to be boyfriend and girlfriend rather than just friends?

Let's assume a relationship has become one of dating rather than just friendship. How concerned should we be? Will our teenagers lose any remnants of reason they had and be ruled entirely by their hormones? It was quite an eye-opener to me to read the research suggesting that, in comparison to their parents, adolescents tend to be more sophisticated when it comes to forming judgements of who is and isn't a suitable partner. In one study, fifteen- to nineteen-year-olds were asked to state what qualities were important in a dating partner. Dependability, considerateness, pleasant nature, and sense of humor were rated as more important than dress. In another study, girls rated the personality of a prospective boyfriend higher than looks. Their parents, however, placed appearance, manner, and conversational skills before personality. This presumably gives an edge to clean-cut, smooth-talking psychopaths.

When we acknowledge both the changes that have taken place in boy-girl relationships in adolescence and the qualities teenagers value in others, we can feel somewhat more confident that our sons and daughters will make sensible decisions when it comes to dating relationships. They want a lot more than a means of expressing themselves sexually; in fact, most teenagers rate the sexual component of a dating relationship as far less important than other aspects of the friendship, such as understanding, affection, and respect. Of course, their choices will not always be good ones and they may need our help to avoid or end relationships that are clearly harmful. But their goals for relationships seem commendable.

While I believe we often tend to be overly anxious regarding dating relationships, I am not advocating a total permissive approach. In keeping with the discussion of parenting styles, I see dating as providing a great opportunity for discussion and negotiation. A first requirement would be top marks on the sex education "course" referred to earlier in this chapter. The next step would be to establish guidelines and limits. Do you expect to meet the girlfriend first? How much will you be told regarding where they are going and with whom? What nights can they go out? How often? Should there be a curfew? I suggest to parents that they raise these questions with their children before they show an interest in dating. This is helpful in two ways. The first is to establish the expectation that dating, like many other matters, will be discussed and negotiated openly. The second is to provide reassurance that limits and guidelines will be in place. Dating relationships may be exciting, but they can also be a source of anxiety and pressure. Knowing that parents will retain some degree of control can avoid the stress that having too much freedom too quickly can bring.

While we're on the topic of anxiety and stress, the subject of dating is a must for sharing your own experiences. For many of us, the prospect of dating fed into our worst fears as well as our favorite fantasies. Being turned down, not knowing what to say, and having to coat yourself with antiperspirant before you even thought about engineering a first kiss are not exactly treasured moments. But I am a great believer in getting as much mileage as possible out of the painful lessons of our past, and I have a veritable wealth of nonexperiences to draw on when it comes to dating.

Without knowing it, I must have had a way of communicating over the telephone that ensured girls would not feel worried or pressured by any reluctance to reject me. They turned me down without so much as a moment's thought and most didn't even have the decency to stifle their laughter. But after allowing my bruised ego to recover, I would try again, knowing that sooner or later I would catch someone off guard and get the arrangements made before they came to their senses. So eventually Joan became my first girlfriend, and I know to this day that deep in her heart she truly loved me, even though word got back after we broke up that she thought I was a lousy kisser. What really hurt was that she told everyone exactly why I was such a lousy kisser. Being in a state of near panic I apparently shook and trembled so hard that it was like kissing a jackhammer.

Teenagers sometimes don't know that their parents have had to deal with the same concerns, heartaches, fears, and disappointments that they face. I encourage my children to see the humor in their father's struggles as an adolescent in the hope that they will be more accepting of theirs.

SEVEN

School, Work, and Play

WE HAVE A SON WHOSE BODY CONTOURS ARE PERFECTLY matched to those of couches and armchairs. By Saturday afternoon we often feel the need to give him a poke to upgrade his condition from coma to semistupor. Once we get him up and doing something, he has energy to spare; left to his own devices, however, he would soon view operating the channel changer as forced labor.

One important part of children's development is to reach the point where they no longer rely on others to energize and direct them. Children seem to acquire these internal controls at different rates, and a common concern for parents is that their son or daughter is not showing the drive and motivation needed to achieve success.

School: Leading Horses to Water

IT WOULD BE HARD NOT TO HAVE LIKED MARK. THIS sixteen-year-old had an easy, pleasant manner and a keen sense of humor. He obviously had a relaxed attitude to life and this was driving his parents to distraction. Each semester his typical pattern was to coast for the first couple of months, warm up very slowly after experiencing the fallout from his mid-semester report card, and then work with modest enthusiasm to ensure that he at least passed some of his courses. The frustration for his parents was that they were certain he could achieve higher grades. They also knew that, unless his marks improved, his chances of being accepted at a college or university would be negligible and they wanted him to have this option.

Parents often share this type of concern regarding school achievement, and understandably so. It continues to be the case that the higher the level of education reached, the better are the young person's prospects in the work force. While there is some truth to the idea that there has been a glut of college graduates in certain fields, the unemployment rate for those who complete post-secondary education remains lower than for those who do not. One factor is the shifting pattern in the demand for different types of occupations. For example, the number of jobs available to un-skilled industrial and farm workers has declined and is expected to continue to do so. The need for people with technical and profes-sional qualifications, however, has increased in many areas.

Mark's parents wanted to know what to do. Their question was simple: "How do we get him to work?" I have been asked this question in various forms by many parents and I dread it. Re-sponses such as "Beats me" or "That's a really good question—I wish I knew the answer" do not enhance my reputation. When confronted with this issue, I suggest a checklist that the parents might use to determine if there are additional steps that could be taken to support and direct their teenager's education.

Number one on my list is the question of determining realistic expectations for school performance. Mark's parents saw him as bright and so they were convinced he could do well if only he would work harder. In most instances parents have no reason to question their judgement, but situations can arise in which the expectations for young people exceed their potential. Although the issue is complex, I do believe there are innate differences in intelligence: some children are quicker to learn than others. Of course, the quality of the environment—and in particular, the extent to which parents and teachers stimulate and challenge the child—will have a very important role. But it is still the case that for some children learning comes more easily.

We tend not to make the distinctions between children in terms of their intelligence that we did several years ago. Whatever terms were actually used, this early categorization of children sadly left some feeling slow or stupid, while others thought of themselves as the cream of the crop. We are now far less inclined to label children; we are also less prone to failing them in elementary school. One consequence is that, by the middle school years, there can be a very large range in abilities among the students in a particular grade. It would not, for example, be at all unusual to find a grade-eight class in which there is a student who can read as well as most adults and another who is barely literate. As a consequence, grade placement may tell very little about the actual level of achievement.

My suggestion to Mark and his parents was that it would be helpful to postpone meeting as a family and arrange individual testing sessions to obtain a profile of his abilities and potential. Like most young people, Mark enjoyed this process and, at the end of all the tests of intelligence, memory, aptitudes, and interest patterns, I was able to give him a reasonable picture of his relative strengths and weaknesses. This type of information can be useful when planning both a high-school program and considering possible career directions.

I had to break the news to Mark that he did well on the testing. I told him I had no choice but to tell his parents that he was not only quite bright, but also possessed an excellent memory. These findings would only confirm their view that he was underachieving. We discussed a possible bribe. For a modest sum I could tell his parents that his potential was unfortunately limited in the hope that they would no longer nag him about school work, but we were unable to agree on terms, so the truth was revealed.

But not all students end up with profiles like Mark's. Over the years I have seen a number of young people whose intellectual and memory skills are below average and who are trying to contend with course work that is just too difficult for them. A student taking grade eleven advanced courses whose intellectual potential and basic academic skills are in the bottom 25 percent of her age group will almost inevitably be finding it very hard, if not impossible, to obtain acceptable marks. When discussing such results I raise the difficult but important issue of revising expectations for achievement. Obviously we want to avoid selling students short by setting expectations too low. This can create a self-fulfilling prophecy: that is, if young people are led to believe they cannot reach a certain goal, this lack of confidence can lead to their failing to achieve in situations where success might, in fact, be possible. At the same time, if expectations are too high, the frustration associated with feeling overwhelmed by school work and experiencing repeated failures can damage self-esteem severely and foster increasingly negative attitudes towards education. Some middle ground needs to be established so that students can both utilize the skills they have and experience success. This may mean taking a reduced academic load or transferring to courses that are less demanding academically.

I should also mention specific learning disabilities. Students with such disabilities are of at least average intelligence and some are very bright. For reasons we don't yet understand adequately, however, they have a specific area of weakness that interferes with their progress. This "learning block" can create a puzzling picture. Kim began avoiding school in grade eight. Her first approach was to develop aches and pains and use these to persuade her parents to let her stay home. When this strategy was no longer effective, she began acting out by refusing to hand in assignments and occasionally taking off from school without permission. Kim's report card typically indicated that her rate of progress was slow and that she had particular difficulty with written work. Just talking to Kim, however, was sufficient to tell you she was bright. She used her extensive vocabulary articulately, and it came as no surprise to learn from her teachers that, in spite of her academic difficulties, she could be a star in classroom discussions.

Kim did very well on the intellectual assessment. It was painful for all concerned, however, to give her the test of writing skills. The girl who had no difficulty holding her own in conversations with adults could not construct a sentence or spell words that had been part of her spoken vocabulary for years.

Kim's specific learning disability was in the areas of symbolic language and visual-motor integration. All this meant was that she had specific weakness when it came to connecting sounds to letters, as well as having difficulty with the mechanics of printing and writing. For Kim and her parents, knowing that the problem was due to a learning disability came as a great relief. Kim was not underachieving; she was not lazy and didn't have a bad attitude. She was a bright person with a disability that was no one's fault. Efforts could now be concentrated on developing a program consistent with her learning disability, such as including more oral examination, providing remedial tutoring, and teaching her how to use a word processor.

The second item on the list is to explore study skills. Some students seem to develop these naturally; others don't. Our first two children were perfect illustrations. Joanne organized her notes, started working on assignments in plenty of time, and would plan when to study before a test. Tim was a different story. Our greatest fear was that the state of his notebooks might reflect the state of his mind. To this day he swears he was the only student in his high school never to have been given an examination schedule or more than twelve hours notice that essays and projects were due.

While achievement is still valued highly in North America, our study habits generally seem weak in comparison to other cultures. For many European and Japanese students, for example, three to four hours of homework a night is not unusual. By comparison, the results from one North American study tell us that less than one-third of students spend an average of an hour or more studying each night. Forty percent report that they typically do no homework whatsoever.

Many students get by for years with poor study habits and skills. Sooner or later, however, they may find that their natural intelligence is no longer sufficient to get them through. They need to become more organized and efficient, but lack the skills to do so. I like to ask students what approaches they use to taking notes from classes or books and how far in advance they set up a timetable for studying. Blank stares are far more common than answers and make it clear that foreign concepts are being introduced. This can promote a discussion regarding how the necessary skills could be acquired. Many excellent books and programs are on the market that make study skills quite easy to learn and apply. Libraries, bookstores, and especially guidance departments at high schools are all potential resources for information and materials. And parents can help provide the structure that may be needed by younger high-school students. Negotiations regarding how much time your son and daughter should set aside for studying each night may be long overdue. If they protest and start to claim that you're robbing them of their childhood, threaten them with boarding school in Tokyo or Geneva.

As for number three on the list, I advise a modified version of the "Don't you know the value of an education" lecture. I emphasize the term "modified version"; in its standard, unabridged form it is likely to evoke only eye-rolling, sighs and passive indifference.

The discussion should be tailored to the teenager's aspirations. First of all, be assured that most adolescents have the types of goals and ambitions that would meet with their parents' approval. Several studies have indicated that young people's job aspirations either reflect or surpass their parents' level of achievement. It also seems to be the case that these aspirations remain fairly consistent. If their goals do become more modest, it is usually because the students become more realistic—for example, acknowledging that a career in engineering is probably not feasible if math is a relatively weak subject.

So the typical problem is not one of an absence of goals, but rather lack of information regarding how these might be achieved. When students don't have this information it can be hard for them to truly appreciate how important their performance in their current courses may, or may not, be. For example, I have talked to young people who do not understand that obtaining papers for the skilled trades often requires passing fairly tough examinations as well as gaining practical experience. I have also met other students who do not realize that law involves postgraduate training, which requires an undergraduate degree, which, in turn, requires obtaining the level of marks needed to enter university. The object, therefore, is to inform young people so they can reach their own opinions regarding the value of an education. Some parents will be able to provide their daughter or son with the type of information they need. Many will not: it is hard to keep abreast of the changes in the educational system or to know what jobs are out there and how to qualify for them. This is where career counseling comes in, and many see this as a process that should start early in high school.

The objective of career counseling is not to slot teenagers into particular occupations, but to give young people the facts needed to make them aware of how their current choice of courses and level of achievement can influence the range of careers open to them as they reach adulthood. One study involving over thirty-two thousand high-school students found that two-thirds of eleventh graders had never received any career guidance. This situation seems to be changing for the better, but it may still be necessary for parents and their teenagers to take the initiative in obtaining counseling through the high-school guidance department, career counseling services in the community, or their own research, using materials available in career sections of libraries and bookstores.

The fourth and last item on the checklist focuses on teenagers' emotional well-being. Are there family difficulties that are interfering with school? For example, it's hard for students to concentrate on their work if they're worried that their parents might be splitting up. Is a girl chronically unhappy because of problems with peers? Could a boy's avoidance of school be related to drug or alcohol abuse? If it seems that difficulties of this nature are present, the task is not so much one of getting the young person to work, but addressing the problems that stop them from working. This can require family or individual counseling or other mental-health services.

So let's say your daughter has "passed" the checklist. She's bright enough to succeed, has appropriate study skills (or the opportunity to acquire them), is aware that a fifty in grade nine Latin will not guarantee a place in medical school, and is as psychologically stable as her age and your spouse's family background will permit. What steps can you now take if she continues to be "on strike" at school? Referring back to that old saying about horses and water, perhaps there comes a time when you have to acknowledge that the water is there in plenty and you've done all the leading possible. The last step is not one for you to take.

My mother decided I was a horse when I was sixteen. After lamenting the fact that the law forbade her to send me to the glue factory, she acknowledged that I would have to find out for myself if an education was important. Eventually it did become extremely important to me, but that was after several years and many jobs.

I am always careful about sharing my history with families. First of all, they have not come to see me because of any interest in my life. Furthermore, I don't want to convey the message that dropping out at sixteen is a good idea. At the same time, once young people have an awareness of their potential and have the opportunity to use this, parents have, in my opinion, done their job and done it well. If their son or daughter is of school-leaving age and continues to use high-school as a cross between a drop-in center and a retirement home, I ask them to consider employment as an alternative to education. I can fully appreciate why parents are often reluctant to do this. They know that not having a high-school diploma will be a very significant obstacle to finding more than a menial, low-paying job. But staying at school and doing next to nothing doesn't exactly prepare you for the work force, and it may even teach you that being clothed, fed, and watered is your birthright and that you have to do absolutely nothing in return. Most young people will develop sufficient self-motivation to sustain them through high school and beyond. For those who don't, I believe little can be accomplished by nagging them repeatedly.

Mark left high school at seventeen without a diploma. I continued to meet with the family intermittently after the decision to leave school had been made. The term "leaving school" was used deliberately—not "quitting" or "dropping out." Mark was going to try something else and his parents were there to offer support and encouragement. Mark's task was a hard one. It took a lot of searching to find work, and after paying for room and board, all his clothing, and other necessities, he was not enjoying the lifestyle to which he wanted to become accustomed. Although it was difficult, his parents continued to support his decision and vowed never to say anything close to, "We told you it wasn't easy out there." While enduring deep teeth marks on their tongues was painful at times, they concentrated on what Mark was achieving, knowing how important it would be that they not see him as a failure and communicate this view to him.

I will have to disappoint those of you who are waiting for a happy ending. I don't know if Mark ever decided to return to school, although he still has very many years to continue his education if he so chooses. As we had discussed with him, brain cells do not rot—at least not for many decades past your teens. If it becomes important enough for him in meeting his goals, he may well decide to use the potential he knows he has to succeed in the educational system.

Work: Does It Build Character?

THE IDEA HAS A CERTAIN APPEAL: PUT STUDENTS TO work in their spare time so they will become more responsible and have less opportunity to be led astray. In the past, people have been very supportive of this view that part-time employment will build character, and some psychologists have even prescribed work as an antidote for adolescent rebellion. The hope was that, by placing teenagers in jobs where they would have to take on adult responsibilities, they would put aside any thoughts of challenging authority that might have been lurking in their minds. It sounds great, and believe me, if employment were proven to make young people more compliant, I'd be donating three members of our household to the work force tomorrow. But, as usual, things aren't that simple.

The issue of student employment is particularly relevant for parents in North America. The number of teenagers working while attending full-time education has risen steadily. For example, in 1940 under 5 percent had a part-time job. During the last decade, however, surveys have indicated that 80 percent will be employed at some point during their high-school years. At any one time, approximately half of eleventh- and twelfth-graders are employed.

Not only is the incidence of employment much greater, students are also working longer hours. In one study it was found that over half of senior students who had jobs were working more than fourteen hours a week. Another survey indicated that over half of a similar group of students held at least the equivalent of a half-time job.

How much character-building actually goes on? Like many parents, we had hoped that our oldest child would mature when she got her first part-time job. In a way she did. Joanne's supervisor at the local library was very pleased with her. She was always on time and I remember how stunned we were to see her up and presentable at eight o'clock on a Saturday morning. And later when she was working in a donut store, we learned how readily she followed instructions and took the initiative to see that her work was completed as expected. After a while our pleasure and disbelief turned to mild resentment. We realized she was definitely growing up, but not for us. If she had adopted the same approach to her job as she usually did to her household chores, customers would have been eating day-olds by the time they were served or, during a particularly bad stretch, would have been in danger of wearing their Boston creams.

We were not alone in finding that the work habits and attitudes demonstrated on the job did not generalize to other areas. When groups of students have been studied, the results have failed to show a higher level of responsibility among those who are working. Perhaps it is simply a question of choice. If you want to keep a job, you either know or learn very quickly that you really have no option when it comes to following instructions. "I'll do it later" or "Why should I?" do not get you very far with employers. At home, however, such lines can be a standard introduction to the type of debate and conflict that most families experience at some time or another.

Another argument for part-time employment is that it helps students acquire work-related skills. To some extent this may be true, but only in a very limited sense. Having the responsibility of a job may help young people learn to organize their time more effectively. Most of the jobs held, however, involve largely repetitive and manual activities, like stacking books on library shelves and serving coffee and donuts. The types of skills learned will not typically be of much help to the student in pursuing the kinds of career goals that most set for themselves.

But if they work, you may think, they will be saving for their education or, better still, so they can look after you in your golden years. This is highly unlikely. Saving accounts may be opened, but for the most part these are no more than temporary holding places.

It is your local retail and entertainment industries that are reaping the benefits; some 80 percent of students spend all or nearly all of their earnings indulging their short-term goals and whims. They buy stereos and clothes, go to movies, and eat a lot of fast food. I can still recall how enjoyable it was to first have this type of financial freedom and power, and I do not begrudge others this pleasure. But it remains the case that most adolescents do not handle money in ways that would objectively be more sensible, such as setting aside a portion as an investment for their future.

At this time I should state that I will not try to convince you that teenagers should not mix school and work; this is a matter that needs to be decided on an individual basis, taking into account factors such as the number of hours to be worked and the young person's academic abilities. Problems can develop if the student is working relatively long hours; the danger zone seems to begin somewhere between fifteen and twenty hours a week. Grades tend to decrease and students are likely to pick courses that are less demanding and potentially of less value to them. Furthermore, the likelihood of leaving school before graduating increases significantly. Not unexpectedly, it is the marginal students who are at greatest risk. If they are already struggling with their courses and putting in a twenty-hour work week, it is of no surprise that their grades begin to suffer.

Alcohol and drug abuse are also higher among students who work long hours. Why this is so is unclear, but premature affluence and the more ready access to alcohol and drugs that this brings could be factors. It may also be that the stress and boredom often associated with long hours of routine, menial work increase the likelihood that teenagers will look to drinking or drugs for excitement.

While research has its limitations, the results to date have not confirmed the belief that part-time employment typically has beneficial effects for students. This doesn't mean that teenagers should not work. If right now your daughter or son is out of the house slinging burgers or pumping gas, I recommend you do no more than enjoy the peace and quiet. The only caution would be that parents and teenagers need to be aware of how important it can be to balance work and school. Provided the hours of employment are not too high, I would not be concerned about the possibility that part-time work would expose them to unnecessary risks. This may be particularly true for younger teens; parents of ninth-graders seem to generally approve of their daughter's or son's employment. As students get older, however the need to balance school and work may become more critical, as it is the senior high-school students who are typically facing tougher academic demands and who tend to work longer hours. For them, employment is more likely to be associated with problems. Parents can find themselves worried about the degree of independence that has been obtained, conflicts regarding use of money and leisure time can arise, and signs that school performance is slipping may develop.

When our younger children reach adolescence we will probably encourage them to have at least some involvement in the working world. But this intention is no more than a matter of personal preference; it does not reflect any belief that it will be primarily for their own good. Our expectation will be that they assume some of the responsibility for funding their lifestyles. At the same time, we know a family in which the parents have a very different point of view. Their three sons have not been allowed to work at all during high school and, in keeping with what we know from the research, they are far from showing any signs of being irresponsible or overly dependent.

Play: Pets, Jazz, and Patriotism

WORK DOESN'T NECESSARILY BUILD CHARACTER, BUT what about play? During adolescence young people begin to make choices regarding use of leisure time that often prove to set the pattern for their recreational lives as adults. For example, over fifteen hundred high-school students who had taken part in a study of leisure activities were reassessed when they were in their fifties. Those who had been heavily involved in sports, artistic activities, intellectual pursuits, or formal organizations tended to maintain this involvement into middle age.

There are some findings suggesting that, overall, young people who are actively involved in social and recreational activities are less likely to display major problems in the community. There are also some data indicating that both involvement in team sports and participation in volunteer activities can have a favorable impact on self-esteem and social development. But we do not know very much about the extent to which a particular type of leisure activity has any positive influence on other areas of life. Rest assured that the research is on its way. I particularly like the article "Juvenile Jazz Bands and the Moral Universe of Healthy Leisure Time," published in the journal *Leisure Studies*. The title guaranteed I would read on. The author talked about the positive influence of becoming involved in an organization such as a band; he claimed, for example, that it fosters self-discipline and even patriotism. Get them signed up!

But my all-time favorite is entitled "Common Leisure Activities of Pets and Children." Adolescent pet owners (at least those in Germany, where the study was conducted) read more than those who do not. My first inclination was to advertise this research and buy a pet store. Then I continued reading. Pet owners are also more likely to visit discos. "Why?" you may ask. Like you, I will have to wait for the next instalment to find out, but I share the concern I'm sure you now have regarding the likely fate of those innocent gerbils, dogs, and goldfish whose owners had upset their parents by frequenting the local discotheques.

Although we know very little about the effects of particular leisure activities, they do provide a way for young people to increase their range of involvement with peers and the community in general. The need for adolescents to begin separating from the family and establish their own identity will be discussed in the next chapter, and developing recreational interests can probably be an important part of this process. Somehow I am doubtful that pet ownership (or lack of it) will prove to be a hallmark of well-adjusted youth. I would wager, however, that activities teenagers find both interesting and challenging, and that require cooperation and responsibility, will be found to have beneficial effects. Until I learn otherwise, I am preregistering my youngsters for the high-school band and basketball.

EIGHT

Push Comes to Shove

The Need to Break Away

CHILDREN GET VERY LITTLE PRIVACY. IF OUR FIVE-YEAR-old is alone somewhere in the house and quiet (a rare occurrence) we tend to suspect that something is going on and will launch an investigation. If our two-and-a-half-year-old is alone and quiet we *know* there is something going on and have learned that the "Whatever you're doing—don't!" approach is best, even though the assumption of guilt may seem like trampling on her civil rights.

We don't allow young people very many opportunities to be away from us. During their early years they remain extremely dependent on the family. For the eighteen-month-old, the home can be a dangerous environment. She can fall down stairs, tumble off furniture, pull pots off the stove, choke on small objects, and slip in the bathtub. We child-proof our homes as best we can, but keep our toddlers close to us most of the time.

As they grow up we probably provide fewer opportunities for them to be away from adult supervision than has been the case in previous generations. I really did walk over a mile each way to school at the age of five (okay—I did have shoes and it wasn't through snowdrifts). Sometimes I walked alone and sometimes with a friend, but never with an adult. Back in the fifties, parents did not have the concerns about child abduction and abuse that trouble us today.

Ensuring that children are rarely far away from adults is, of course, not only motivated by the wish to protect them. There are also many things they cannot do for themselves. Consider the eighteen-month-old again: she needs someone to change, wash, dress, and feed her. Doors need to be opened, toys have to be lifted down from shelves, and books have to be read. And while we encourage children to become more independent, the idea that they require our help rightly persists. Showing them how to use a spoon is replaced by trying to teach them what to eat in order to be healthy. Instruction regarding dress progresses from doing up their own buttons to how to dress for school and not invite ridicule.

Eventually we need to become far less involved in teaching and directing our offspring. By the time they leave school we want them to have reached the point where they are ready to live independently. This requires a process of separating in which adolescents, in some respects, push away in order to decrease dependency on parents. As reliance on the family decreases, so teenagers become more involved in the community in which they will be expected to function independently in a few years.

Separating involves establishing an identity. Being a distinct and unique person becomes very important, as does belonging to other groups apart from the family. Without these bridges, leaving home can be a frightening and lonely prospect.

The task of separating is also quite complex: it requires achieving independence and developing strong ties to the community on one hand, while maintaining some connection to the family on the other. This task is accomplished in a number of different ways.

Cliques, Crowds, and Friendships

PEER GROUPS SERVE A CRITICAL ROLE IN PREPARING adolescents for independence. In order to learn more about the way teenagers group themselves, field researchers have gate-crashed parties, attended rock concerts, and eaten countless burgers in fast-food restaurants. I make no attempt to mask my envy and admiration of social scientists who have managed to get agencies to fund reliving their adolescence; as a result of their dedication we know more about the way teenagers group themselves and how these groupings tend to change over the course of adolescence.

One distinction made is between "cliques" and "crowds." Cliques are tight social groups that have relatively few members. The emphasis is on intimacy; a forum is established for sharing opinions, exploring feelings, and providing mutual support. Developing close relationships outside the family can, however, seem very threatening. You need to know that you will be safe if you let down your guard and begin allowing others to see your doubts and insecurities. So membership in cliques is regulated pretty carefully. This is fine once you're in, but obtaining membership can be difficult. First of all, cohesiveness gets harder to maintain if the clique is too big, so you may have to wait for a vacancy. Secondly, any would-be members have to be screened meticulously to ensure they have similar interests, values, and social standing. We use the term "cliquish" to refer to the more negative aspects of this type of grouping—in particular, the cold and sometimes blatantly unkind ways members of cliques treat outsiders. The positive side of such groups, however, is that they provide a way for adolescents to gain acceptance, support, and status outside the family.

Crowds typically consist of a number of cliques. Their function is different, with the emphasis being on social and recreational activities. Not surprisingly, crowds usually convene on weekends and can provide the basis for gatherings such as parties.

Much larger groupings also exist that have a looser structure and less well-defined membership. One high school was studied in which four major groupings emerged—jocks, motorheads, brains, and chewers. The first three are self-explanatory. In case you're wondering about the chewers, they were the students who liked to watch, rather than play, sports; listen to country music; call each other on CB radios; and chew tobacco—and could do all at the same time. Those not identified with any of the four were described as "in-betweeners."

In addition to providing a sense of belonging and status, investment in groups outside the family provides a way of gaining social skills. Teenagers learn how to talk to different people, form judgements about others, and establish themselves in a particular hierarchy. They may want to experiment with being a leader and can find more opportunity to do this in peer groups as opposed to their families. They learn about dating relationships and begin exploring what they want in a partner, as well as gaining insight into what they have to offer a potential mate.

Finding the right group—and getting into it—can be hard work. Teenagers may temporarily join a group just to see how comfortable they are in it. They may move between cliques and crowds until they find the types of relationships and activities that are satisfying and enjoyable to them. This can take time and can be very frustrating if they don't feel they belong anywhere. In my early teens I recall trying out for the jocks; I may have lasted an afternoon. Why people would voluntarily seek opportunities to get out of breath, sweat, and ache all over was, and has remained, quite beyond me. At that point I disliked school, so I didn't even apply to be a brain.

Research has also looked at the changes in the importance of group membership over the course of adolescence. The pressure to belong to cliques and crowds usually becomes strong in early adolescence and reaches its peak in the mid-teens. By the time they are entering adulthood, and presumably feeling somewhat more confident about themselves, the groupings often become much looser. For example, rather than definite cliques and crowds, there is more likely to be a number of couples who tend to get together socially. This pattern of interacting is one that persists throughout adulthood.

Peer groups can exert a lot of influence on young people; there is a strong pressure to conform, and parents can become concerned that this pressure may be negative. It can be very worrying to realize that you have far less control over their friendships than was once the case. After all, there was a time when you almost always knew where they were and with whom, as well as enjoying veto rights over birthday-party invitations and guest lists for sleep-overs. Now they want many of their social activities to be well away from the home and you realize there is a significant part of their lives from which you are excluded.

I have always taken some comfort from the studies that have looked at the criteria adolescents use for selecting friends. The chapter on sexuality touches on the research that examines this issue with reference to dating. When it comes to broader friend-ships, it seems that teenagers also place value on qualities that I am sure most of us would applaud. For example, in a study in which teenagers had a choice of over five hundred personality character-istics to describe the ideal qualities for a friend, the four that were picked with the highest frequency were sincerity, honesty, under-standing, and loyalty. That's a pretty good profile. Of course, adolescents may make poor choices at times, but most learn from such mistakes and continue to seek to establish the kind of friend-ships and group affiliations that will help them develop in positive ways.

A World of Their Own

WHEN I FIRST MET ANDREA I SHARED HER PARENTS' VIEW that she seemed depressed. She had little animation and there were few signs of any emotional reaction to what she or other people were saying during the interview. At home she also seemed to be very distant. Her mother, in particular, had noted how often Andrea would stay in her room alone. She would have preferred to have eaten meals on her own if this had been allowed, and she rarely expressed any interest in going out with the family.

It took quite some time to reach the point where Andrea would discuss more than superficial matters with me. As I began to know her, however, I came to appreciate that there were at least two reasons for her apparent withdrawal. The first was in keeping with her parents' perspective: Andrea was feeling unhappy about a number of matters. In this respect, spending time on her own could be seen as a symptom of emotional problems. At the same time, her solitude had a practical and valuable purpose. It was allowing her to undertake some thoughtful and necessary self-analysis and problem-solving. Her major problem was that she had not yet found ways to deal with the fact that she disliked her teacher and was not very popular at school. She used much of her time alone to try to figure out why she was having these difficulties and to plan what she might do about them. She brought her diary in to one session. It was full of suggestions she had for herself—almost like blueprints for action. My role became to act as her planning consultant and I saw no reason to discourage her from spending time alone. I also encouraged her parents to view it as working in her room rather than retreating.

From studies of how adolescents use their time, we know that they are alone for approximately a quarter of their waking hours. This is a quantum leap from the amount of time young children spend on their own. So what are they doing? Believe it or not, a major pursuit seems to be constructive thinking. I am sure we can all remember times in our lives when we have been faced with more change than we anticipated or more uncertainty and confusion than we felt able to handle. For most people, taking time to reflect, analyze, and plan is automatic. If we don't do this, we can be faced with the negative consequences that often follow rash and impulsive decisions. Adolescents are in much the same position— probably even more so because of being in a period of rapid and far-reaching change. They need to explore different ways of thinking and behaving. As one developmental psychologist, Paul Mussen, put it, "Adolescents need time to integrate the rapid changes occurring in their bodies and minds into a unified sense of identity." It sounds like heavy work, and it is.

When teenagers get behind closed doors, there is a chance they may actually be working, although I admit that it's hard to know. Someone lying on a bed with a glazed expression might be in the throes of an existential dilemma, but they could also be goofing off. I suspect most adolescents indulge in both extremes, as well as many points in between. For the most part, however, I recommend to parents that they give their teenagers the benefit of the doubt. Unless there are indications of problems such as depression, the need for solitude can be seen as healthy rather than as a sign that something is wrong or that parents and other family members are being rejected.

Regardless of what teenagers may actually be thinking when they are on their own, just having a physical space or territory that is theirs can help establish a degree of independence. We make great use of territory in our society. Having your own office, for example, is often a sign of having reached a certain status. And the more status you have, the bigger your office. This does not have to make any sense from the functional perspective. Bosses and supervisors rarely need a larger work area than their subordinates, but you would be surprised to find the president of a company in a small corner office.

Having their own space can be equally as important for adolescents, and the bedroom is the most likely territory to be involved. I had to share a room with my brother for many years.

John was always far more organized than me and he laid out clear guidelines and regulations regarding which areas were his and which were mine. He was older, wiser, and stronger—the perfect combination for giving him an edge in the negotiations regarding how to divide the territory. I recall that I had my bed against the far wall and a thin track that allowed a path to the door. But these were *mine* and I was happy. We eventually moved and I had my own room. I can still remember how excited I was to have four walls and a door that was just my own. A declaration of independence quickly followed; I wanted no one else to enter my territory unless they had my permission. This declaration was not met with any resistance. While I believe I was always loved, nobody in the family was overwhelmed by grief or loneliness when I took myself off to my room, closed the door loudly, and did my own thing.

Just as a bedroom can become a symbol of adolescent independence, it can also become a battleground. I have heard countless horror stories over the years. One family was almost reduced to eating straight out of the cooking pots until they discovered that their son had full table settings for at least a dozen people hidden in various piles of papers and clothes in his bedroom. The daughter who literally could not remember the color of her bedroom carpet will also never be forgotten.

I have always been reluctant to become involved in the Battle of the Bedroom. Without wanting to go overboard in analyzing the symbolism, some teenagers use the bedroom as a means of asserting their need to make their own decisions and rules. From this perspective, not adopting house rules regarding neatness and cleanliness is a relatively harmless way of establishing a degree of independence from the family. Whenever my opinion is asked for, I recommend one of those hydraulic hinges that ensures the door is always shut (to be bought by the teenager in question). I also suggest that the parents no longer take any responsibility whatsoever for their son's or daughter's laundry. If they would rather throw a clean item of clothing in the general vicinity of the laundry basket than take the trouble to put it away for future use, let them rewash it. If they have no clean shirt or blouse for the school concert or have nothing to wear for the party, the old standby "Tell someone who cares" may not exude empathy, but it covers all that needs to be said. They can have their privacy and establish a territory all of their own; they can also have full responsibility for the consequences of not managing their territory efficiently.

Youth Culture and the Generation Gap

THE NOTION OF A "YOUTH CULTURE" HAS BEEN USED TO describe one way in which adolescents attempt to establish separate identities for themselves. The assumption is often made that the values, beliefs, and priorities teenagers take on are very different from those of adults, resulting in a generation gap. The term "gap" also adds the idea that the separation between teenagers and parents is a result of irreconcilable differences: we don't understand them and they don't understand us.

How real is the generation gap? Sometimes it can seem like teenagers have become aliens. The way they look, speak, and act can seem incomprehensible in light of the fact that you have shared the same gene pool and home environment. When you consider their tastes in music, dress, hairstyles, and vocabulary, it seems impossible to escape the conclusion that they must be under the influence of outside forces. Yet in other respects there may be less of a gap today than existed in the past. The sixties did bring a certain counterculture, with groups of young people subscribing to ideas that were clearly at odds with those of the establishment, such as use of psychedelic drugs, commune-style living, and free love. But more recently there has been far less evidence that parents and teens differ with respect to their value systems. One way of studying this matter is to look at the sources of advice and potential influence adolescents turn to when making decisions. Do they sit at our feet ready to catch the pearls of wisdom we cast in their direction or do they seek counsel from their friends in the belief that we are out of touch, old-fashioned, and otherwise irrelevant?

Inevitably it seems that the results of the research are mixed. Where adolescents look for advice depends very much on what particular matter is being decided. Let's start off with areas in which we are defunct. When it comes to questions such as dress, other aspects of personal appearance, choice of recreational activities, and appropriate hours of sleeping, we lack a certain credibility in their eyes. I can live with this. In fact, there have been periods when I wanted this fact to be advertised: when Joanne and Tim were teenagers I had absolutely no wish to be seen as having any responsibility for the way they looked at times. But what about other areas of decision-making? When adolescents are presented with problems regarding money, education, or career plans, it seems they typically attach more importance to parents' opinions than those offered by friends. Furthermore, other research has failed to find the differences between young people's values and those of their parents that would be expected if there were truly a large generation gap or distinct youth culture. When issues such as drugs, education, work, and sex are explored, the attitudes held by adolescents and parents tend to be similar, and certainly more so than was the case in the seventies.

While teenagers are more oriented towards their peers than preadolescents, it seems that this is not necessarily accompanied by a rejection of adult values. When choices have long-term implications, teenagers are particularly likely to give more weight to the views of parents than to those of their peers. Parental style also has an important role to play here. When a more democratic style has been adopted, parents usually retain greater influence over their teenagers' decisions during adolescence. One study of mothers and daughters, for example, found that mothers were more likely to be seen as role models by their daughters if they were not perceived as being rigid and authoritarian.

None of the above means that your teenager should be sitting at your feet waiting for those pearls. Chances are they already know your views on most topics and could recite many of them word for word. Also, they have lived with you for many years and see your values reflected in your day-to-day actions. They cannot help but know how much importance you place on ideals such as commitment to work, loyalty to family, equality of the sexes, and moral obligation to help the disadvantaged. The occasions on which opinions actually need to be sought or given may be few.

Pushing away does not typically represent a real rejection of parents. It is more likely to be a phase in which teenagers take what they have learned from the family and begin applying it to the world in which they will soon have to be independent.

Letting Go

WHILE MOST OF US DO NOT FIND THAT OUR LIVES BECOME meaningless after our adolescents have flown the nest, the process of separating isn't always easy. A teenager's task is to move away; ours is to let go, and this can be every bit as hard as theirs. In many ways the depth of our attachment to our children is unique and would be hard for them to understand. They were almost totally dependent on us for many years, and we have felt a sense of caring and responsibility for them that they will probably not experience until they become parents themselves.

I can remember becoming aware of the fact that my teenagers were no longer discussing certain areas of their lives with me. I understood why, but it took a while to feel comfortable with this distance. Every once in a while I would suggest that if they did not want me to know what was really happening in their lives, they could at least make something up so that I would feel informed. I also let them know that if they wanted me to feel really happy, they could invent a problem, seek my advice, and pretend to be impressed by my wisdom. But after a time I stopped being so concerned about the fact that they had become less dependent on me. I started fantasizing about what life would be like when they left, and I must admit that the fantasies began to have a certain appeal.

Sometimes the strength of the attachment parents have to their children can be matched by the strength of their resistance to recognizing the need to let go. The signs of this resistance are often easy to detect. I have seen many a teenager wince and sigh when their parents refer to themselves or each other as "mommy" and "daddy." They may be equally put out by the kindly smiles forthcoming in response to their views and complaints. To the adolescent this can be reminiscent of the amusement that young children's comments and ideas often evoke. Of course, teenagers can contribute equally to the problem. Just as being treated as a twelve-year-old when you're fifteen can create conflict, so can trying to act like an eighteen-year-old. But for now I'm picking on us parents. We need to give our teenagers the opportunity to move away and try things out for themselves. They will reach the stage when they have the right to make their own mistakes: this was a right mine exercised liberally.

Tim had a way with cars. He passed his test shortly after his sixteenth birthday. It was his first attempt. Nothing to do with talent I assure you: the examiner who took him through his paces simply wanted to ensure that the experience would never be repeated.

It took Tim at least three years before he realized that an automobile was a potentially dangerous machine and should be treated with more respect than a bumper car at the fairground. Don't misunderstand me, we were intent and serious in our efforts to instill in him a healthy respect for the automobile. As he had heard more times than he cared to remember, I have had the opportunity to see the tragic effects of car accidents more than many people. But there always comes a time when you have to stand aside, cross your fingers, and worry while your son or daughter begins to learn first-hand the lessons you wish they could learn directly from you. So Tim was allowed to drive the car.

Tim left the late movie one night and decided to take a short cut from the parking lot to the main road home. He set off only to find that what he thought was a small lane was a footpath. This footpath disappeared, leaving Tim driving over wasteland. Tim, always an astute and perceptive person, realized he would be in trouble if the police noticed him, so he proceeded to turn his lights off. It was not a bad move to avoid detection, but chances were also good that Tim would not spot anything either—such as the large boulder that destroyed the underside of the car and allowed our mechanic to discharge his second mortgage.

What can you do? You can get mad. You can remove driving privileges. You can insist that your daughter or son pay for the damage. You can lecture. We did all of those things. But eventually we let him drive again. We did not make him wait very long either. Our decision was that we would prefer him to have the opportunity to learn how to drive responsibly as soon as possible. In many respects it was no different from the anxiety we had experienced when he rode his bike. I swear children think they are immortal. I wish they never had to do anything even remotely dangerous. I wish we never had to sit at home and worry while they test their wings. We worry both because we love them and because we know they can get hurt—sometimes badly. So we do our best to prepare them. The rest is up to them, just as it was for us in our day.

Test Yourself: The Letting-Go Quiz

PSYCHOLOGISTS HAVE A WEAKNESS FOR QUESTION-naires. You name it and one of us has invented a scale to measure it. Romantic love, quality of life, and even fear of fat have been reduced to one of those pencil-and-paper, fill-it-out, and find-the-truth-about-yourself-in-under-three-minutes quizzes. Here is my contribution to the field of psychological testing; just by answering these questions you can discover if you are in need of major surgery to separate from your offspring.

---

1. I liked living with my child when she was   True   False
    nine. I will like it four times as much
    when she is thirty-six.

2.	Children who leave home before they are forty are impulsive and rebellious.	True False
3.	I believe it is my responsibility to support my child until he is eligible for a pension.	True False
4.	Peter Pan is an ideal role model for children.	True False
5.	My child would be as the proverbial lost sheep without my guidance.	True False
6.	Having a child and receiving a life sentence are one and the same.	True False
7.	There's no one else to shovel the driveway and mow the lawn.	True False
8.	If my child left home she would eat nothing but macaroni and die of scurvy.	True False
9.	My child has to stay at home to meet my need to be punished.	True False
10.	My life would be empty without the bother, aggravation, and poverty that caring for my children brings.	True False

If your True score is under 3, you are well on your way to enjoying the empty nest. Between 3 and 5 suggests you could have a struggle; every once in a while you will probably throw a wet towel on the floor, cover the kitchen counter with crumbs, and leave all the lights on just to remind you of the old days. Anything over 5 is hopeless; you might as well resign yourself to terminal parenthood and begin negotiating what kind of curfews and limits will be appropriate for a forty-year-old.

The Gentle Shove

WHAT IF YOU ARE READY TO LET THEM GO AND YOU can't get rid of them? Tracey was a nineteen-year-old who was in urgent need of leaving the nest and I take some pride in knowing that I had a hand in her launching. She did not enjoy living at home, and the lack of pleasure was mutual. Her parents commented and complained about the incredible transformation that seemed to take place as she walked up the driveway. In the community she acted like an adult, but by the time she was through the front door she seemed to have regressed to early adolescence. Her parents could not understand how she could act so responsibly at work, but still needed to be reminded about the expectations and routines that had been established in the home for years. The amount of room and board to be paid was hardly more than nominal, but Tracey seemed to be viewing it as extortion. She argued that she needed to save as much as possible in case she decided to go to college, although her lifestyle suggested her savings account was in sorry condition.

I do not want to paint too negative a picture. Tracey appeared to be a friendly, warm, and capable young woman. It was just that she needed to move on and had not. Her parents had considered the idea of telling her to leave, but it had not led to any action. Their concern was that Tracey would feel rejected and they felt guilty just at the prospect of insisting that she spread her wings.

I have learned that you cannot stop parents from feeling guilty. They are the world's leading authorities on the subject. They can blame themselves for anything and everything and their favorite question is "where did we go wrong?" Having come to accept that parents need a certain amount of guilt, I try to capitalize on this emotion rather than fight it. So I suggested to Tracey that she sue her parents and that it would only be fair if they give her the money to do so. (I have to admit I like getting people's attention, and this worked very well.) The reason for the lawsuit was very simple. Tracey's parents had failed to provide the necessities of life.

They were teaching her to be dependent and were robbing her of the opportunity to gain self-confidence and self-respect. She would never learn how to manage a realistic budget or run her own household. As a result of her parents' neglecting her needs, she would soon be brainwashed into believing that she could not cope with the adult world on her own.

Tongue-in-cheek ideas can sometimes have an impact and we subsequently spent several sessions debating the notion of whether or not it would be an act of kindness, as well as self-preservation, for the parents to insist she leave home. Tracey was obviously hesitant about this prospect; the predictability and comfort of home life can become addictive. But eventually a plan was made. A date for the launching was set and her parents decided to make this a special occasion—a true celebration of her moving on. When I met with the family later I was pleased to hear that Tracey had at least made some effort to make her parents feel like "schmucks" for "kicking her out." It just doesn't feel right when teenagers go along with their parents without mounting some resistance.

This story does have a happy ending. The last session was just after the first dinner Tracey had cooked for her parents in her home. I'm sure the evening will be remembered as a signal of their new adult-to-adult relationship. Her parents even did the dishes without being told.

NINE

Who Are the Experts?

SEVERAL YEARS AGO I BEGAN BROWSING IN SECOND-hand bookstores and inevitably found myself drawn to the titles relating to my field. Soon I had a modest collection of long-forgotten books about child-rearing, and for the first time, I began to see the value of studying history. Like several of my fellow students, the reason for having to take this subject at school had always been a mystery to me. So it was a genuine surprise to find myself finally agreeing with my teachers' insistence that there were important lessons to be learned from the past.

The most valuable lesson for me was becoming acutely aware

of how easy it can be for people with professional qualifications to believe they are truly experts. I read books by authors who were understandably seen as prominent members of their professions. They had graduated from established universities, held responsible positions, and were obviously highly respected members of society. Yet many of the beliefs they held and much of the advice they offered would be seen by most of us today as nothing short of ridiculous. They were not frauds or quacks who were bent on deceiving the populace for personal gain. They were sincere and well-meaning people who had the best interests of children in mind when they wrote. To illustrate my point I would like to return to the Victorian era and present a few examples of what the experts were saying.

Storks, Gooseberry Bushes, and Other Fables

I CAN'T REMEMBER WHEN I FIRST ASKED ABOUT HOW I came into this world. At some tender age I probably expressed an interest in the subject. I do recall that my brother had a burning desire to find out where I had come from, but only because of his wish to send me back.

I also can't remember what type of reply I typically received when inquiring about baby-making. Like many of us, I recall hearing about storks and finding babies under gooseberry bushes. Perhaps I once believed these fables, but does it really matter? Telling young children that they came by airmail may be a trifle silly, but is it any more outrageous than trying to convince them that a large man loves children so much he squeezes down millions of chimneys in a single night to give them presents, or that a rabbit hops around the world leaving jelly beans and chocolate eggs?

One hundred years ago the indifference I have expressed about such fables would have been attacked vehemently by the experts. I'm not talking about an honest disagreement or a lively debate as to whether or not children should be given the truth rather than a fairy story. To the experts I would have been seen as a very dangerous person and as someone who should never be allowed to publish his views.

The Victorians had a certain passion that we seem to lack. Once they believed something they were unshakeable. Because of grave concerns regarding lying, one prominent physician and writer began contemplating how this characteristic might develop. First of all she used the cardinal rule that mothers are the best targets whenever an expert wants to lay blame. (In case you didn't know, they have single-handedly caused schizophrenia, autism and, I suspect, athlete's foot and the hole in the ozone layer.) So it came as no surprise to learn that mothers cause the problem, or to quote: "Nearly everyone who is now grown up got his (or her) first lesson in lying at his mother's knee." And what might this lesson be? Storks and gooseberry bushes, of course. Such myths penetrate the subconscious, and the child "receives a mental warp and injury which nothing can ever eradicate entirely." You can try to make it up to them, but no number of anatomy and physiology lessons or diagrams of the reproductive system can undo the damage you've caused.

Let's say that you were a wise and knowledgeable parent who had never made mention of storks or gooseberry bushes. But had you been teaching them nursery rhymes? Another expert was ready to pounce on you. This time the problem was not that you were giving them false information. (After all, dishes do not elope with spoons and the chances of blackbirds singing after being baked in a pie are pretty remote.) What you would be doing, however, is stunting their growth. "How?" you might ask. It's simple: memorizing nursery rhymes sends too much blood to the brain and diverts the "nerve-force" from its primary duty of organizing physical growth. Overtaxing the mind in this way guarantees that harmful effects will follow. So if your son or daughter is below average height, take a hard look at yourself. How many times did you sit down together with the Mother Goose books? Was it really worth it? Any chance of ever making the basketball team was wiped out just because you thought it was cute to have them recite Humpty Dumpty for grandma.

The level of guilt and fear generated in parents must have been high. If you were one of those parents who had overtaxed your child's brain, the prospects were not good. You read on to learn that "if the life of the child be spared, the future is liable to be blighted by a general want of strength and by disorders caused by a defective nerve-force."

Before leaving the Victorians, I want to go back to the topic of legs. It wasn't until I read Dr. Rankin's *Hygiene of Childhood* (1890) that I understood that covering legs was more than just a reflection of modesty. Cold feet meant increased blood flow to the higher regions of the body and hence greater risk of pelvic congestion. This, in turn, it was stated, created a risk of inflammation and death. The habit of wearing only slippers in the house was, therefore, extremely hazardous to health. Insisting that daughters wear shoes, woolly socks, and flannel drawers was seen as nothing less than a life and death issue.

It is easy to be critical when you have access to an extra century's worth of information. My criticism of the Victorian authorities on child-rearing, however, is not that they were wrong; it is that they acted as if they had exclusive access to the truth. They claimed that they were simply passing on the laws of nature that parents would disregard at their children's peril. They rarely offered their statements as views, opinions, or theories: they knew the truth and parents had better listen.

Have things changed? In some ways I believe they have. People in the child-care field tend to be far less dogmatic than their Victorian counterparts. There is more discussion of "approaches" and less insistence that the ideas being offered are laws of nature. In other respects, however, the myth that the truth has been discovered lingers. For people such as myself the myth is great for business. If the truths about child-rearing have been established, then you would expect psychologists and the like to have at least the most important ones at their fingertips.

When I was studying experimental psychology, I recall being advised that social scientists should be ambitious and bold in what they attempt, but modest in what they claim. I like to keep this advice in mind whenever I consider the field of child psychology—and in particular, child-rearing. Conducting research that is valid and relevant is so hard to do. All of us would love to know the best way to raise our children so they grow up to be well-adjusted members of society. But could we ever agree on how to define a term such as "well-adjusted" in the first place? Just how should success be measured when it comes to being a parent? Is it in terms of our children's academic or vocational achievement? If so, what is the best way to measure achievement? With respect to academic success, is it just the level of qualification that matters? But what about effort and motivation? Do we want to think of a young person who worked very hard to reach grade twelve as less successful than a gifted student who coasted through college with mediocre marks? And what about success in the working world? What are the measures to use? Salary level? Number of employees under your control? Contribution of the work to society?

You might decide to focus more on children's personality and emotional development. Immediately the problems with definition resurface. What are the important personality characteristics? Does being a warm, sociable person count more or less than being an assertive individual with leadership qualities? What is more worthwhile—feeling a strong need to achieve or having a content and relaxed attitude towards life?

One last problem has to be mentioned. Even if we could agree on how to measure children's success or adjustment, it would be very difficult to know for sure what actually caused them. The way parents treat their children undoubtedly has a major influence on their development, but so do many other factors, such as heredity, school, peer groups, and the prevailing culture. Trying to untangle all these effects and determine how much each has an impact on the way we are as children and adults has always been a major headache for social scientists. Given the readiness with which the experts have responded to children's problems by convicting parents without even considering other potential culprits, I feel obliged to make a contribution to correcting the imbalance. I accept full responsibility only for those things my children do that could be seen as successful; all else is the result of the combined influences of their mother's genetic legacy, the alignment of the stars at their birth, and their kindergarten teachers.

To my mind, the state of our knowledge is far from the point where people in my field can come close to being able to present themselves as experts who hold the key to successful parenting. At best, we can act as consultants to families and can justify offering this service on two counts. The first is that, because we spend much of our daily lives talking to children and parents, we hear a lot about the issues that create conflict and about the steps families are taking to try to make things better. As we offer suggestions and listen to theirs, we learn which ones tend to work and which ones are not so useful. In other words, we learn from the experiences of working with families in the same way that all adults learn from carrying out their daily responsibilities.

The second reason for believing we should still be allowed to practice in spite of my insistence that there are no real experts is that we should be keeping ourselves familiar with the studies that have been conducted in the field. While I may have poked fun at research (including my own), I do hope that social scientists will continue to get their grants and will add to our understanding of human behavior. I personally find their results helpful. I have been impressed enough by the research into parenting styles that there is no way our youngest children will be given the opportunity to have the freedom that their older brother and sister enjoyed. I am also convinced that I worked too hard in "teaching" values to my teenagers. Chances are that we have laid the foundation of our children's moral and social thinking, for better or worse, by the time they reach adolescence. Chances are also good that, whether or not they actually talk to us about their major decisions, they do attach weight to our opinions. So while Aaron, Kiera, and Alexandra will be denied the experience of going to school wearing swimsuits over their clothes, they will probably be spared most of my standard, overused lectures when they reach adolescence.

I encourage parents to seek ideas and suggestions. I would never, of course, discourage them from buying books about teenagers; there are even some suggestions at the back of this book as to which ones they might purchase. The self-help sections of bookstores have grown in size and contain many titles relating to child-rearing. There are also audiotapes and videotapes that discuss topics such as communication, discipline, and sexuality. Community groups sponsor speakers and workshops to increase parenting skills and phone-in shows offer advice for specific problems. To top it all off, you may have the benefit of grandparents who will, at no cost, provide a regular report card and summary of what you should be doing. Before I get in deep trouble, I want to state publicly that I always appreciated my mother's approach. She argued that, if she had been an effective model of how to be a parent, we would follow suit and she would have no reason to intervene. On the other hand, if she hadn't done such a good job, she would be the last person who should give advice to the next generation of parents. Either way, we could count on her respecting us as parents.

Having listened to all the advice—invited and otherwise—parents will always be left with the most critical step. Only they have the knowledge that is needed to decide what particular action will best meet the needs of their daughter or son in a given situation. Research and theories in the social sciences can never take full account of the vast range of individual differences among children and young people; that requires a depth of understanding and sensitivity that only comes through years of sharing your life with someone. Parents may not often feel like experts, but sometimes the people most qualified for a job are the last to know it.

Suggested Reading and Tapes

Acker, Loren, Bram Goldwater, and William Dyson. *AIDS-Proofing Your Kids: A Step-by-Step Guide.* Hillsboro, OR: Beyond Words Publishing, 1992.

Bayard, Robert and Jean Bayard. *How to Deal with Your Acting-Up Teenager: Practical Help for Desperate Parents.* New York: M. Evans and Co., 1983.

Bell, Ruth et al. *Changing Bodies, Changing Lives: A Book for Teens on Sex and Relationships.* New York: Random House, 1980.

Coloroso, Barbara. *kids are worth it! Giving Your Child the Gift of Inner Discipline.* New York: William Morrow, 1994.

——— · *Winning at Parenting* (audio tapes). kids are worth it!, P.O. Box 621108, Littleton, CO 80162.

Dinkmeyer, Don and Gary McKay. *Parenting Teenagers.* New York: Random House, 1990.

Greydanus, Donald et al. *Caring for Your Adolescent.* New York: American Academy of Pediatrics, 1991.

Guh, Beverly. *Teenage Years.* Tucson, AZ: Fisher Books, 1989.

Mayle, Peter, *What's Happening to Me?* New York: Carol Publishing Group, 1975.

Nelsen, Jane and Lynn Lott. *Positive Discipline for Teenagers.* Rocklin, CA: Prima Publishing, 1994.

Planned Parenthood. *How to Talk with Your Child About Sexuality: A Parent's Guide.* New York: Doubleday, 1986.

Index

About the Author

Dr. Peter Marshall is a father of five, a child psychologist, and a resident of Barrie, Ontario. Although born in England, he lived for two years in the Far and Middle East, and finally moved to Canada in 1973. He has worked in the field of psychology for the past two decades either as a university professor or a practicing clinician, and has also appeared on radio and television discussing his views on sexuality, assertiveness, teenagers, and step families.

MORE PARENTING BOOKS FROM PRIMA PUBLISHING

Positive Discipline for Teenagers:
Resolving Conflict with Your
Teenage Son or Daughter
by Jane Nelsen, Ed.D., and
Lynn Lott, M.A., M.F.C.C.

You don't have to be perfect to be a
good parent. And you don't have
to have perfect children. This
book shows you how to turn off
the cycle of guilt and blame and
begin working toward greater understanding and communication
with your adolescents.

"I highly recommend this book to
parents, teachers, and all others
who work with young people. It is
one of the best books I have seen
on helping adults and adolescents
turn their conflict into friendship."

—H. Stephen Glenn
Co-author of *Raising Self-Reliant*
Children in a Self-Indulgent World

Setting Limits: How to Raise Re-
sponsible, Independent Children by
Providing Reasonable Boundaries
by Robert MacKenzie, Ed.D.

Most parents have difficulty striking the right balance between permissiveness and restrictiveness.
They are frustrated and discouraged by their child's misbehavior,
but they can't seem to do anything
about it. Robert MacKenzie has the
answer. His three-step method
helps parents teach their children
how to make acceptable choices
and understand the consequences
for unacceptable behavior.

ORDER FORM

Quantity	Title	Unit Price	Total
_____	*Now I Know Why Tigers Eat Their Young*	$12.95	$_____
_____	*Positive Discipline for Teenagers*	$14.95	$_____
_____	*Setting Limits*	$10.95	$_____

7.25% sales tax (CA residents only) .... $_____

Shipping ($3 for the first book, $1.50 for each additional book) .... $_____

TOTAL ORDER .... $_____

How to Order

By telephone: With VISA/MC, call (916) 786-0426 Mon.-Fri., 9-4 PST.

By mail: Just fill out the information below and send with your remittance.

I am paying by (check one): ☐ check ☐ money order ☐ VISA/MC

Name (printed) _____

Address _____

City/State/ZIP _____

VISA/MC # (if applicable) _____ exp._____

Signature _____

Prima Publishing
P.O. Box 1260
Rocklin, CA 95677

♦ *Satisfaction Guaranteed!* ♦